GOOD NEWS FOR MUSLIMS
TOOLS FOR PROCLAIMING JESUS TO YOUR NEIGHBOR

John F. Haines

Middle East Resources

Philadelphia, Pennsylvania, USA

Published by:

Middle East Resources
PO Box 96
Upper Darby, PA 19082

Telephone: (610) 352-2003

Rights for publishing this book in other languages belongs to Middle East Resources. For further information please contact the publisher at the address above.

Library of Congress Catalog Card Number: 97-071236

ISBN 1-881085-01-5

Cover Design and Photo: Chris Leaman
Printed in the United States of America

This book is dedicated to the memory of my colleague and beloved brother in Christ, Bill Saal. My prayer is that many will follow his example and become faithful witnesses to Muslim friends whom God places on their path.

"This is the message God has given us to pass on to you: that God is Light and in him is no darkness at all."

1 John 1:5 (Living Bible)

Contents

Foreword

He was certainly a bit unusual, sitting there in a small Midwestern town cafe, drinking his coffee and reading an Arabic newspaper. When I asked, "Is that an Arabic newspaper?", he seemed pleased that someone would be interested, and we began a conversation. He was a student at the university nearby, and came from a Middle Eastern country closed to proclamation of the gospel. I should add that I don't read Arabic nor did I feel particularly comfortable talking with Muslims. I had occasionally seen how my friend John Haines loved these people for Christ's sake, however. I observed that he enjoyed talking with them no matter where he found them. As I talked with the young man I remembered John saying that Muslims love to hear and tell stories. So after a while I said, "I'd like to tell you a story." He indicated he was interested. I continued, "It's a famous story about a father and his son. Jesus told it to teach us what God is like." The young man listened respectfully as I told the story of the Prodigal Son. I explained that Jesus taught that God loved us like that father loved his son. Then, just as John Haines had indicated, the young man reciprocated with a story from his background, to which I also listened.

Later I reflected on my unexpected conversation. Missionaries would give a great deal to talk about the gospel with someone from that young man's country. Yet it was I, a lay person living in a Western country, who had the opportunity to befriend this student for Jesus' sake. There are many Muslims living in Western countries who are open to friendly discussions and long to meet anyone who will show interest in them and their background.

Do you have such opportunities? Would you benefit from helpful information about Muslims and how to reach out to those you meet in everyday situations? If so, this Toolbox is for you! The author and his wife have decades of experience with Muslims and the goal of the Toolbox is to enable you to more effectively befriend a Muslim for Christ. So, sit back and soak up helpful information gleaned from countless conversations over meals and cups of coffee, in shops and apartments and on the streets of life. And then — isn't it time for coffee? You never know whom you may meet!

John Stanford

Professor of Physics: Iowa State University, Ames

Using This Guide

In the summer of 1992, my wife, Margy, and I decided that we would do some window shopping in one of our favorite cities: Washington, DC. Our old friend, Al, proved to be an excellent guide as we visited a new mall. Suddenly our eyes focused on a little shop with a French name. We entered and felt right at home with the many items from France. The biggest surprise, however, lay ahead.

I noticed that the man working in the shop looked like an Arab. Gingerly I tested the terrain in conversation. "Where do you come from?" "France." "Oh, so do we; what country did your parents come from?" This was a polite way of not identifying a second-generation young person with his parents' culture. "Morocco," came the friendly reply. We went on to explain that we, too, had spent our first five years overseas in that lovely country. "Where did you live in France?" "Oh, you may not have heard of it: a city called Toulouse." In fact, this is where we lived! The final "coincidence" was that our new friend's name was Abdullah, the same name as a young believer we knew well in our city. He even knew the location of the believer's church.

Arabs appreciate kindly interest in them and their culture more than most other peoples I have met. We went on to share with Abdullah our faith in Christ. He listened politely and accepted some gospel literature. He seemed genuinely touched by God's planned meeting in such an unexpected place. Shortly after this we met an Arab young man at a church conference in Washington. He wanted to know more about our work. I asked him: "Would you like to go and meet Abdullah and take him a Bible in Arabic?" He did not hesitate, and not long afterward carried out his "mission."

How many people of Muslim background has God placed around or near you? Some of them may be American converts to Islam. Others are from families who have immigrated from a Muslim country.

Not long ago I joined in a discussion with a number of Christians of different nationalities. Some were lay people, others were workers who were supported by local churches. Our concern focused on how we could reach the masses and hidden clusters of Muslims scattered all over Europe and other Western lands. We concluded that the people we need to train are not foreign workers but local Christians.

Pastors are seldom on the front line of witness to Muslims. Our prime mandate is to train church members. This sounds unexciting. But I am convinced that more Muslims will come to Christ as lay people in the West are trained to reach Muslims around them. In Western countries Christ has built local congregations with Muslims on their doorsteps. In all of these, church members hold the key to the often-closed hearts of their Muslim neighbors.

Does this seem simplistic? Perhaps even revolutionary? The men and women in the pew remain the most effective witnesses. Are these not the ones Christ commissioned at the end of Matthew, Mark, Luke and John? Were not *all* believers designated in Acts 1:8? "But you will receive power when the Holy Spirit comes on you; and you will be my witnesses in Jerusalem, and in all Judea and Samaria, and to the ends of the earth."

My objective in writing is that this "toolbox" would be biblical, practical, transmissible, and targeted.

Biblical, because only the power of God's Word can cause the truth to be born by the Holy Spirit deep within the heart of our Muslim neighbors. In every chapter the reader will find many Bible truths to help sort out the complexities of Islam and the Muslim's religious practice.

Practical, because questions which Muslims use to challenge us often do not reflect the issues that tug at their hearts. My prayer is that Muslims, the ones in your path, will come to know Jesus as Savior through the help you will find here.

Transmissible, because many of the concepts you will learn can be used directly with your Muslim friend. This communication may take place over a kitchen table or on an assembly line or in an office. The believers God has planted in these places need to reach out to their Muslim friends in Jesus' love.

Targeted, since this guide is intended as a communication tool for reaching Muslims living in a Western country. Many of them live in a seesaw world. At times they swing up into the Western lifestyle around them. At other times, they swing down into the world of their families. My wife and I lived in North Africa for five years and make frequent trips there. Today we live among North Africans in Europe. These experiences help us to understand the tensions of Muslims living between two cultures. After all, we do too.

There is a secret weapon for waging spiritual warfare in bringing the Good News of forgiveness to Muslims in the West. This weapon is the Christian who lives and works alongside Muslims. As you begin working through this manual, you may feel unqualified and inadequate. You may hesitate to speak of your Savior to someone as different as a Muslim. This feeling actually shows that you have fulfilled the first qualification for witnessing to Muslims: *I cannot, but God can*.

We will begin by examining the vital place of prayer in seeing our Muslim friend find the Good Shepherd. Prayer is the first and fundamental tool to be used in each aspect of our witness. The first tools you will learn to use are what I call *Basic Tools*. One of these is a relevant, coherent presentation of the gospel. This will help you be God's co-worker. The Bible's teaching on Arabs is like the arrowhead on the shaft of our message. Then we will learn to use the *Finishing Tools*. We will try to understand our friend's immediate world, a world very different from our own. Then a chapter deals with the religious world, to help in the spiritual warfare necessary in combating the occult practices of popular Islam.

Let me comment briefly on some of the resources I used to develop these ministry tools. Qur'anic references in the text are taken from the edition printed in Tunis under the title *al-qur'an al-'aDHiim, wa maktabatiha*. A more useful edition for the non-Arabic reader is M.H. Shakir's parallel English and Arabic Qur'an. Unless otherwise noted, all English Bible quotations are from The New International Version (Grand Rapids: Zondervan Publishing Company, 1984). Arabic Bible references are from the older Van Dyke version. Today's Arabic Version (TAV) is a popular, more recent translation. It is available for the whole New Testament and is best for someone learning Arabic. Other colloquial Arabic translations that are useful are *kitaab al-'ahd al-jadiid li-rabbina wa-mukhalliSina yasuu' al-masiiH* (The New Testament). This so-called Mogrebi Arabic version is in Colloquial North African Arabic, as compared with the Modern Standard Arabic (MSA) version (sometimes called Classical Arabic).

Generally, the TAV and MSA translations are becoming more satisfactory, as those who read are learning to do so in MSA.

I want this guide to be a tool in your hands. You will find help here in communicating your faith to Muslims in a coherent, heart-reaching way. A carpenter knows that the best tool is one that is familiar and tested. My objective is to provide tested tools that you can use immediately in your witness. In this way, you will build a unique portion of God's House. As you become skilled in using these tools, you will delight in Christ's presence at His return. Your former Muslim friend will be right at your side to meet the Lord Jesus.

1

Prayer

No effective evangelism can progress
against the great stronghold of Islam
without the heavenly view
brought by worship and prayer.

This manual presents you with a set of tools. You should find them helpful in testifying of your faith to your Muslim neighbor. I believe that anyone witnessing to Muslims will discover what I do continually. The tool to which I return most often is prayer.

Imagine that you are building an object from rough wood. You work from a preconceived plan, a design. You want to get into the mind of the designer. In our case, the designer is our Father in Heaven. God directs the final appearance of our work in the people He brings across our path. We work with them through His Spirit's skill. God also designed the individual tools for the building process. These are the principles of evangelism set forth in the Bible.

In prayer we discover both the Master Plan and the method. All of the other tools depend upon our effective use of this fundamental tool. Without prayer, our construction project will get off to a very poor start.

Prayer and Worship

At the very heart of prayer we find the biblical doctrine of worship. We bow before our great and holy God, our Father. We come before God on behalf of our Muslim friend. Then we speak. Our communication is at risk of being garbled almost immediately, however. Why? Because of the very different concepts of worship in Islam and Christianity.

The Muslim Creed is fundamental to what any Muslim believes. It states: "I testify that there is no God but Allah, and that Muhammed is the Apostle of God." Here, as elsewhere in the Qur'an, the names of God and Muhammed are placed side by side. No other prophet receives such honor in Islam. Yet our friend claims to believe in the equality of all prophets under God. This link of the name of Muhammed with that of God is seen often in the Qur'an.[1]

We need to realize that the Islam we discover through Muslims is usually not strictly the Islam of the theologians. As Christian witnesses, we find a spiritual melting pot of various beliefs picked up by our friend. This is called *popular Islam* or *folk Islam*.

Take the Muslim Creed, for example. These are the first words spoken at a baby's birth and the last words recited at death. With great emotion, an older person present says in Arabic, "I testify that there is no God but Allah, and that Muhammed is the Apostle of God." What is its use in popular or folk Islam? In the actual practice of popular Islam, the use of the Creed can bring the Muslim dangerously close to *shirk*. This Islamic term means the association of another with the one unique God. Muslims may associate Muhammed with God by placing Muhammed's name close to that of God in their devotions.[2] In their devotion for Muhammed, Muslims may practice the very sin they profess to abhor! Ask God for discernment to see where your friend comes from spiritually.

It is of utmost importance at the very beginning of our friendship with a Muslim to do some serious thinking about the nature of worship. What are the implications of our concept of worship? What is the impact of our Muslim neighbor's actual practices of worship?

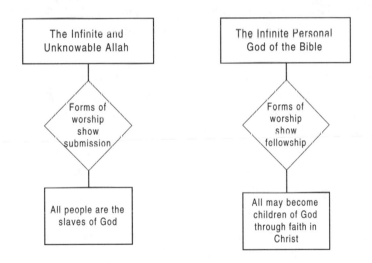

Figure 1: Worship in Islam and Christianity

Remember that worship is central to our use of the tool of prayer. God intended from the beginning of history that we should worship Him and His Son, Jesus Christ. John was the great apostle of the deity of Christ. He shows us Jesus' deity very clearly in the climax of his writings, the book of Revelation. In Revelation 4, we are directed toward the Eternal God, seated on His throne. Worship is offered to Him. The scene suddenly changes in chapter 5. Now the Lamb, Jesus, is on center stage. He also receives worship (Revelation 5:12–14). All of the capacities and achievements of mankind are to be poured out like the ointment of Mary at the feet of Jesus. In the flow of the sentence structure in Greek, suddenly one word stands out: *worthy* (*axion*). Jesus is worthy. Why? "… because you were slain" (5:9). No other prophet, real or imaginary, can claim this. Our Lord Jesus Christ merits the sevenfold offering described in verse 12. He receives "power and wealth and wisdom and strength and honor and glory and praise!" As we grow in worship of Christ and bring this kind of offering daily to His feet, we put on *spiritual armor* for confronting the spiritual Goliath that is Islam. Our hearts focus on Christ in worship. Then we move into action in prayer.

What is our goal in this prayer? We have seen that Christ is not at the center of our Muslim neighbor's vision. Christ will become that vital spiritual focal point only as Muslims center their worship on Him. This is because the Lord Jesus alone is worthy of it as the Lamb of God. As His witnesses, we come to God in worship and intercession. Then God's Spirit breaks up the hard soil of the heart of our friend.

We should never distort worship. We should also beware of *neglecting* worship. One summer a youth team met to prepare for outreach to the many Muslims in a large city. Each morning we aimed at putting on our armor for the spiritual battle. We called it a time of Bible study and prayer. Yet I began to realize that we were falling into a very predictable rut. Our Bible study time would always fill its allotted period. If anything, it would spill over into the prayer period that followed. Little by little, worship and intercession were squeezed out.

Yet "always keep on praying" is the last weapon on the list in Ephesians 6:10—8. Look at the Great Commission itself. In Matthew's Gospel, it is preceded by a time of spontaneous, Spirit-guided worship (Matthew 28:17). How could we have missed the point? Yet we did, and we do. It is essential also to restore the broken walls of worship in our lives.

We must also learn from the culture of Eastern people. In the Qur'anic view of God, one sometimes can almost feel the vastness of the desert that Muhammed and his contemporaries knew so well. *allaahu akbar!* God is the Greatest! This is true. How is your worship; how is your prayer life? Your success depends on it.

During the eight years my wife and I spent in Grenoble, France, I was the only non-Frenchman among the elders of our church. There were many times when we came to our Monday evening prayer meetings burdened with some daily concern. We were sometimes aware of a difference of opinion. Yet there was never any open, lasting breach of unity. The basic reason was that the Holy Spirit had drawn us to Christ and to one another in our worship of Him. Our opening seasons of adoring Christ so often melted us together.

I discover this prayer priority as I participate in various Muslim ministry teams in Europe and elsewhere. We deliberately allow adequate time for worship. In so doing, we guard the centrality of Christ in our life and witness. This is the fundamental secret of shaking the very foundations of *al-umma al-islaamiya*: the Muslim Nation. There is enormous potential for spiritual change in even the tiniest worshiping group.

After the Apostle John tells us that the Lamb is worthy, he spells out in sevenfold detail exactly what this means. "Worthy is the Lamb who was slain, to receive *power* and *wealth* and *wisdom* and *strength* and *honor* and *glory* and *praise*" (Revelation 5:12).

As we wait before our Heavenly Father in worship, often we are led to action. For example, we may be made aware that our riches are not being used in the right way. Perhaps our attitude toward another person has not been honoring to the Lord. God may give us new wisdom in developing a relationship with a Muslim friend.

When I lived in Marseille, France, I was very burdened for the large College of Science near my home. At that time, no open Christian witness existed on campus. I used to walk several days a week on the back road, up to a large metal rear gate to the campus. As I did, I asked God somehow to open the spiritual doors. Then in a very unexpected way, God began to answer. I met two Syrian students in a French class. I then learned to my great surprise that they were good friends of an Arab Christian I knew.

Worship opens spiritual doors. Learn anew to worship Jesus the Son of God. That worship will inevitably reach out to the Muslims whom God, in His providence, has placed at your doorstep.

Now I want to underline three aspects of this vast biblical doctrine of prayer which I have found pertinent to my own ministry in friendship evangelism.

The Conflict of Prayer

Have you ever had this experience? You have just come to the place of prayer. You anticipate beginning a time of communion with the Lord. Suddenly, you remember a little chore that needs finishing. Or a nagging inner voice tells you of the note that you must jot down before something is forgotten. Before you know it, your mind has begun to wander. Suddenly you realize that you have wandered aimlessly down some corridor of thought. We all have experiences like that daily. Why?

The answer is found in Ephesians 6. Paul describes a great battle going on between us and a satanic host of "spiritual forces of evil in the heavenly realms" (Ephesians 6:12). Our victory in the fight involves taking the armor that is provided for us. It also requires us to "pray in the Spirit on all occasions with all kinds of prayers and requests." (Ephesians 6:18). When you begin to intercede, the diversion you experience is a deliberate assault by the Enemy.

Prayer involves conflict! How easy it will be to ease up in your advances against Satan's stronghold in the heart of your Muslim friend. So many good activities will compete for the essential one: prayer. The Lord Jesus Christ must make each of us His "good soldiers" in the incessant daily warfare. Then we become like Paul who said: "For I would have you know in how severe a struggle I am engaged on behalf of you ..." (Colossians 2:1, Weymouth).

The Ministry of Prayer

Does not each of us long to be of some practical use to the Lord? Yet we wonder if our prayers are really important. Do you honestly feel that the time spent before the Throne of God is a ministry?

You may remember reading of Paul's lesser-known friend Epaphras. The Bible tells us that he was "always wrestling in prayer" for the church at Colossae (Colossians 4:12–13). He had a special burden of prayer for those in this small, declining town of Asia Minor. So he worked fervently for them. Where was Paul at the time this was written? In some comfortable office in a seminary? No, he and Epaphras were prisoners in a Roman jail.

Would Paul's restricted circumstances keep him from any kind of a ministry to these Colossians? No, in fact the Apostle had a very real and important work among the Colossians right from a prison cell: "We have not stopped praying for you and asking God to fill you ..." (Colossians 1:9). Epaphras was also active, a real prayer example to us. Paul tells us he was "always wrestling in prayer for you" and "he is working hard for you" (Colossians 4:12–13). Paul and Epaphras, his prayer partner, saw a great work of God accomplished. In that small, distant town they faithfully performed a solid, lasting ministry by prayer.

William Carey once spoke of his field in India as a spiritual gold mine in which he planned to dig. But he was quick to add: "You at home must hold the ropes." Your witness to a Muslim friend is like digging for gold or hunting lost treasure. Yet it must begin with prayer. Prayer is a real ministry, however invisible it may be to those around you. It is certainly neither a waste of time nor an exercise in futility.

The Reward of Prayer

We are often tempted to think that it doesn't really pay to spend time in prayer. There are so many other demands upon our time. Yet our Great High Priest gives us infinite dividends as we come to God by Him. Not the least of these is the absolute delight of actually seeing God answer our prayers. Several days before we first sailed for Casablanca in 1964, my wife and I were reading *Daily Light* together (for April 16). We saw three tremendous Old Testament illustrations of answer to prayer. Pause for a moment to consider Jabez, Solomon and Asa.

Jabez prayed and God gave him protection from his enemies and enlargement of his portion in the Promised Land. Solomon prayed and God so answered that he remains unequaled in human history for wisdom. Asa prayed and God smote a mighty Ethiopian army arrayed before him. Talk about answers! Our prayers often seem quite feeble and faithless. Then we are pleasantly surprised as God repeatedly allows us to see Him specifically answer. Perhaps God smiles then at our low estimate of ourselves … and Himself.

No effective evangelism can progress against the great stronghold of Islam without the heavenly view brought by worship and prayer. This is especially true for the spiritual conflict going on in the lives of our Muslim neighbors. If Christ is not given His proper place, a vacuum is formed deep within a person. Some other person or thing must rush in to fill it.

The first essential tool, then, is to examine the heart of the Designer. We discover what is in the heart of our Heavenly Father through prayer. We enter anew into a ministry of prayer for others. Remember that the ministry that God has given you in prayer is an authentic one. It is just as real as the ministry which He has given you when you are off your knees, talking to your Muslim friend.

For Reflection

1. What are five specific requests I can bring to God for the Muslim He has so graciously brought to me?

2. What prayers of Scripture are particularly relevant to my witness? One of my favorites is Jeremiah 33:3: "Call to me and I will answer you and tell you great and unsearchable things you do not know." Jeremiah goes on to learn from God about very practical matters. God tells him about destroyed houses and palaces. He also enlightens Jeremiah on His refusal to answer the prayers of Jeremiah's people.

3. Is there any key point of spiritual resistance upon which I can concentrate prayer?

For Action

1. Keep a notebook handy as you pray. You will find God will give you real theological gems as you wait on Him. You will also discover practical initiatives as you are before Him in prayer and worship. Don't forget to leave space to write down how God answers your requests.

2. Ask God to give you at least one other prayer partner as you bear witness of Jesus Christ. You might ask a wife or husband or a close friend to pray as you witness. Perhaps a small prayer group in your church will help you not to bear this struggle alone.

For Additional Study

1. Read the biographies of those greatly used of God to reach Muslims: Charles Marsh, Samuel Zwemer, Lilias Trotter and Henry Martyn, for example. Read also about those won to Christ from Islam. Discover what role prayer played in their lives.

2. Keep a list close at hand of verses and passages that help you in your witness. Share these with others, especially your prayer partners. Ask them what God has given them in this spiritual venture together.

2

A Biblical Message

**What message are we to bring
to a new generation of Muslims?
It should be thoroughly biblical,
but also relevant.**

Any lasting work in the heart of a Muslim requires a foundation of prayer. Have you seen a new effectiveness in your prayer life for the Muslim whom God has placed at your doorstep? After prayer, our actual presentation of the gospel is next in importance. It is a very basic tool. Our message must be tailored to their felt needs. These needs stem from the special world in which they live. It is very probably quite different from your own.

We must always maintain a vision for "the regions beyond." The Apostle Paul spoke of this in Romans 15:19–24, where he expresses his burden to reach out in ever-widening circles, like a stone dropped into a pond. Wherever God places us, we must always have in mind the lost masses of Muslims all around us. How will those in your city be won to faith in Christ? The answer is, one at a time. Do not allow church responsibilities or the joys of Christian fellowship to cloud this vision. In reaching out toward your Muslim friend, you share Christ's constant concern. Jesus drove this home in His parables of Luke 15: the lost sheep, the lost coin and the lost son. The *lost* one was the priority.

What message are we to bring to a new generation of Muslims which has grown up in a Western country? It should meet them at the point of their felt need. It should be thoroughly biblical, but also relevant. That which speaks to American, British or French nationals will not necessarily speak to them. The different emphases of the four Gospels remind us that God varies the approach of His messengers. For example, the Gospel of Matthew appears to have targeted the Jews. Its unique form and message focus on Christ as King. Luke, on the other hand, spoke especially to the Gentiles. Its vocabulary reflects this, speaking of Jesus as "The Son of Man."

Modern communication science puts this very well. There must be feedback from the receptor of the message to the source or sender of the message. No feedback usually means no coherent communication. Ask yourself how effective you are in communicating Jesus Christ to your friend. Is the Christian message clearly heard and fully understood?

Through the last few years, Western Christians have been witnessing to their Muslim neighbors in increasing numbers. Working alongside some of them, I began to sense the need for a simple presentation of the gospel to help them in dealing with Muslims. What follows is a plan I have often used in witness to Muslims. This presentation carefully sidesteps minor details that could prove unnecessarily controversial.

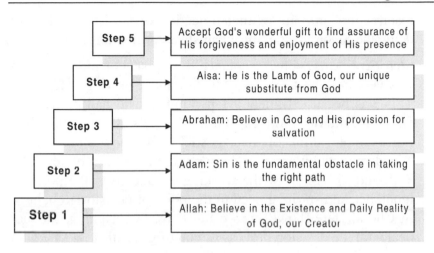

Figure 2: Five Steps on the Straight Path

The plan is very simple: Allah, Adam, Abraham, Aisa,[3] and Acceptance:

Step One begins with Allah: God. Too often we immediately speak of Jesus, without the Muslim realizing how deep and real our belief in *God* actually is.

Step Two is Adam: developing the reality of sin in the story of Adam. Muslims love stories and most are excellent storytellers. In our presentation of Christ we should seek to develop this ability ourselves. Whole families have come to Christ in Muslim cultures through the use of "The Storying Method."[4]

Step Three tells the Bible story of Abraham (also found in the Qur'an, but in a corrupted form). This prepares the way for the sacrifice of Christ, through the near sacrifice and prophetic picture of Isaac.

Step Four speaks of Aisa, the Lamb of God, Jesus Christ. Here we show our friend passages dealing with His death and resurrection. In spite of their rejection of Christ's death and deity, the Sword of the Spirit can slice through unbelief.

Step Five deals with Acceptance of Christ. For many years, I was very hesitant to press a Muslim about making a decision. This was because I knew a fair number who had easily professed for ulterior motives. But the Gospels all stress this fact. For example, think of the Apostle John's powerful cameos: Nicodemus, the woman at the well, the man born blind (John 3, 4, and 9). All show the working of God from the point of ignorance and spiritual need to the point of decision to believe in Christ. Here, however, we must exercise caution. Do not deal with the decision process as you might with someone who has grown up with exposure to the gospel.

Allah: Believe in the Existence of God Our Creator

We see abundant evidence all around us which demonstrates the existence of a wonderful God. He is the One and the Only God — He is our Creator. We observe the powerful heat and light of the midday sun, the stars that twinkle above us in the evening. All these tell us: "God loves you, God created you." God Himself explains this in one of the oldest books existing in the world: the Torah of Moses (*Siidna Muusa*). "In the beginning God created the heavens and the earth" (Genesis 1:1). In six days, God created the heavens, the trees, the sun, animals and humans. "So God created man in his own image, in the image of God he created him; male and female he created them" (Genesis 1:27).

Our ancestor, Adam, was perfectly happy. He spoke with God in the beautiful garden. The conversations Adam and his wife Eve (*Hawwaa*) had with God were their greatest joy. In fact, God created people so that they could have a personal relationship with

Him. We will see that later in the story of Abraham, God's intimate friend. The Torah, and the other books that are contained today in what we call the Holy Bible, all speak without exception about the One and Only God. In the Torah, we read this great declaration made to God's people before the arrival of Jesus Christ on earth: "Hear, O Israel: The Lord our God, the Lord is one. Love the Lord your God with all your heart and with all your soul and with all your strength" (Deuteronomy 6:4).

Jesus Christ said the same thing 1500 years after Moses (cf. Mark 12:29). God said through the mouth of Moses: "You shall have no other gods before me" (Exodus 20:3), suggesting that it is possible that other things may take the place that belongs to God alone. Our thoughts or plans can be made without consulting God, our Creator. We are often interested solely in our own pleasures. We may be preoccupied by a bad habit, or even a prized possession. We may be attached to a car, clothing, or a close friend, more than we are to God. When that happens, we are no better than people who bow down before statues or consult mediums and human prophets rather than God.

The more we see God's glory, the more we see our own sinfulness, our disobedience to Him. God is Almighty. He is also the pure truth, like sweet water flowing from a deep spring in the desert. No one can corrupt or change His Word. God says through David the Prophet: "Your word, O Lord, is eternal; it stands firm in the heavens" (Psalm 119:89).

Adam: Sin Is the Fundamental Obstacle to the Right Path

Adam and Eve possessed everything they needed to be happy. God gave them a perfect garden; yet in that ideal setting God placed a forbidden thing in the midst of the garden. Eve, speaking to the Serpent (the devil in disguise), said: "We may eat fruit from the trees in the garden, but God did say, 'You must not eat fruit from the tree that is in the middle of the garden, and you must not touch it, or you will die.'"(Genesis 3:2–3). Then Satan tricked them. His lie persuaded Eve, and then Adam, that they had been deceived by God. This was how Adam and Eve began to doubt the declarations of the God of truth! We must never forget that every lie we tell has its origin in our refusal to obey the God of truth.

They ate the fruit that God had forbidden them in His love for them. We know the terrible result: "The Lord God banished Adam from the Garden of Eden to work the ground from which he had been taken" (Genesis 3:23). Today, because we are all Adam's children (*abnaa Adam*), we are sinners too. This is not just because we are his descendants. We also have often disobeyed God since our childhood. Every person from every country is a sinner, whatever their religious practices may be. Sin is like a terrible disease that has infected the human race. God Himself says so to us: "All have sinned and fall short of the glory of God" (Romans 3:23).

We will not be able to love God, our Creator, without admitting this painful fact. God Himself declares it. He gave the Ten Commandments to Moses in order to show us His demands. To transgress just *one* commandment would be to make light of God's own person. The Ten Commandments reflect His character. Who could claim never to have disobeyed the last two commandments? They say: "You shall not give false testimony against your neighbor. You shall not covet your neighbor's house … or anything that belongs to your neighbor" (Exodus 20:16–17).

That reminds us of an Arabic proverb: "The net said to the sieve: 'Oh, how big your holes are!'" We so easily speak of the other person's mistakes in order to forget our own. We are just like the net. We are like Adam and Eve who tried to makes clothes of leaves to cover their nakedness. God sees us as we are: guilty of our misdeeds, our sins. Who has never lied about someone else? Who has never been guilty of covetousness, desiring what belonged to someone else?

There is a price to pay for sin, for God is righteous. That price is eternal death, which the Bible calls Hell. There are but two paths that we can take in this world. The first path leads downhill, toward Hell. Those who walk on that path vainly make every effort to pay the price for their condemnation. They forget that it was brought on them by *their own sins*.

God, however, has provided for our salvation by means of a substitute. This is the uphill path that leads upward to God. Those who walk on it believe what He has told them. They receive this substitute.

Abraham: Believe in God and His Salvation

One of the riches of Western countries is their immigrant population. Four thousand years ago, an immigrant of distinction left his own country for Palestine. This immigrant was Abraham, known also as God's friend. An important event occurred late in his life which teaches us a fundamental lesson about the path that leads to God and how to find it.

In the Torah of Moses we read: "God tested Abraham. He said to him, … 'Take your son, your only son … and … sacrifice him … on one of the mountains I will tell you about.'" (Genesis 22:1–2). This son was unique because he was the son chosen by God, although Abraham had another son too. Abraham obeyed. He saddled his donkey and left with his son. After walking for three days, they reached the mountain, with the wood necessary for the sacrifice. At last his son asked him: "But where is the lamb for the burnt offering?" A good question isn't it?

On reaching the place, Abraham bound his son, then he took his knife to slay him. Suddenly the Angel called out: "Abraham! Abraham! Do not lay your hand on the child, and do not do anything to him; for now I know that you fear God because you have not withheld from me your son, your only son." Then Abraham saw a ram caught by its horns in a thicket. He took it and offered it instead of his only son. The next time that you see a sheep being prepared for slaughter, remember the unique Lamb that God provided in your place. We will see that point in the fourth step.

What is the meaning of this old story well-known by many peoples? We have already mentioned that our sins condemn us. Who, then, will pay the price for our condemnation (eternal death according to God's holy law)? Shall we *ourselves* be sacrificed on the day of judgment?

God our Creator does not want us to die in our sins. He found a substitute. This unique person was the only one capable of taking our place. In His love, God sent us His unique replacement. This stirs us to ask: "But what on earth did this replacement do to spare me the eternal punishment I deserve?" This leads us to the fourth step.

Aisa Is the Unique Substitute, the Lamb of God

Up to now we have heard the words of some of the great prophets of God. Now try to imagine the period in which these prophets lived. We will draw a line representing time, with Adam at one end of the line and ourselves at the other. The approximate dates are written underneath; the Torah does not give us a date for creation.

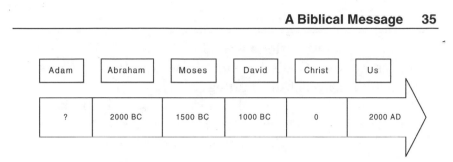

Figure 3: Biblical Timeline

Let us review the steps of Adam and Abraham. Adam showed us the need for a substitute. God showed us a remarkable example of substitution when the ram was sacrificed instead of Abraham's son. Later on, God revealed His law to Moses, commanding His people to bring sacrifices regularly. This was to illustrate the substitution for their sin. In the Psalms (cf. Psalms 22–24), David spoke about the "substitute prophet." This prophet would come after David and would be put to death for the sins of the world. As He was about to die, that substitute of God cried out: "My God, my God, why have you forsaken me?" (Psalm 22:1). Many other prophets also spoke about this great substitute for mankind. It may help to review that step again at this point.

As we saw on the diagram above, the birth of Jesus Christ divides the Western calendar into two ages. His birthplace was in Palestine. At about 30 years of age He began His work of teaching and healing. Jesus experienced continual suffering while accomplishing this ministry. His cousin was also a great prophet – John the Baptist (*yuuHanna al-ma'madaan*). When John saw Jesus, he said: "Look, the Lamb of God, who takes away the sin of the world!" (John 1:29). Why did he give such a name to Jesus? John prophesied, without fully understanding, that three years later Jesus was to be judged by His enemies. They would sentence Him to death. Yet His death was for the sins of the whole world.

The story of Jesus' sufferings in John's Gospel (John 19:1ff.) shows us more of God's love in Christ. The Roman governor, Pilate, took Jesus and had Him flogged. The soldiers mocked and hit Him. On selfish grounds, the most religious men of that time urged Pilate to condemn Jesus. Then a cross was laid upon Jesus. The cross was a horrifying instrument of torture to execute the worst criminals of that time. They forced Jesus to carry His cross as He was led up to the place called "the Skull" or Golgotha (*al-jumjuma*).

God reveals to us that "Here they crucified him, and with him two others — one on each side and Jesus in the middle." He was given vinegar to drink to ease His pain. He refused it. Finally, at the end, He cried out with a loud voice: "It is finished!" The Holy Gospel of John tells us that "he bowed his head and gave up his spirit" (John 19:30). This, of course, means He died.

Can we be sure that it really was Jesus who died on that cross? Yes. We are certain, since both His mother and His best friend were standing at the foot of the cross. They could not be mistaken about Jesus' identity. Moreover, a long time before Christ's coming, God had foretold that Christ was to die — as a lamb sacrificed for the sin of the guilty.

Jesus was the Lamb of God, as pointed out by John the Baptist. Christ died on a Friday. He was laid in a tomb that was sealed by a huge stone and guarded by Roman soldiers. Three days later His enemies as well as His friends were astonished: the tomb was empty! Only the strips of linen that embalmed His body and the burial cloth that had been around His head were still lying there. They were in the same position, but the body had disappeared!

Yes, something extraordinary had happened. Jesus Christ had experienced what no other human being in history had ever experienced. He had risen up again, alive, from the grave, without the intermediary of any other human being. Many saw Jesus Christ during the forty days on earth that followed His resurrection. Then He returned to Heaven. But before that, one of His friends, Thomas, could not believe that Christ was alive again, despite what others had said. He seriously doubted such an unlikely event. He needed proof.

Jesus went through locked doors into an upper room. Thomas was there with the other friends of Jesus. Jesus came toward Thomas and spoke to him. It was at that moment that Thomas recognized the resurrected Jesus. He bowed down before Christ, exclaiming: "My Lord and my God!" (John 20:28).

Through His death, Jesus paid the infinite price to free us from our sins. He became the Lamb of God *par excellence*. God raised Him up from the dead. In this way, God showed that He accepted that the life of Jesus be sacrificed instead of ours.

Accept God's Wonderful Gift of Forgiveness

Here you will find assurance of God's forgiveness of your sin and then enjoy His presence forever. This is the most important step (*al-khaTwa al-muhimma*). There is a children's song about the Messiah that was very popular some years ago. It says:

> One door and only one
> And yet the sides are two.
> I'm on the inside.
> On which side are you?

Jesus said: "I am the gate; whoever enters through me will be saved" (John 10:9). All you must do is to accept by faith the four truths we have just seen. Believe Jesus by taking Him at His word. Then you will be ready to take this fifth step. It is not without cause that we call this "the most important step." This step will enable you to enter through the door of salvation. Jesus Christ Himself is that door. He said so Himself. Are you convinced that God who created you is both truth and love? In His truth He must condemn you because of your sins. In His love He found a replacement, a substitute.

Jesus Christ took your place, the place of a condemned sinner, when He died on the cross. It is to offer you salvation and resurrection for eternity that He triumphed over death on the third day. He did that for you, and He is expecting that you accept Him now. The moral code teaches us that the least we can do for someone who has granted us a great blessing would be to offer him our friendship and our love.

Jesus was the only one who could give His own life in exchange for ours. He underwent an excruciating and unjust suffering on our behalf. What does He ask us to do in return? He asks nothing but what the Messiah reveals to us through the Prophet John in the book of Revelation 3:20. It is Jesus Christ who says to us: "Here I am! I stand at the door and knock. If anyone hears my voice and opens the door, I will come in and eat with him, and he with me."

Few people would refuse to receive their best friend at home. They would even joyfully open the door of their house to welcome him. Would you like to open the door of your life to receive Jesus within? This is the same Jesus Christ who gave His life for you. If you wish to do so, say this prayer:

My God, I thank You for having created me in Your love, and having kept me alive to this very day. Yet I acknowledge before You that I have often been disobedient or even rebellious. I am a guilty sinner. Nevertheless, I believe that Jesus, the Lamb of God, took my place. He died as my substitute, and I believe, because He rose from the dead, that He is able to give me eternal life. Thank You, Lord Jesus, for Your love. Please come into my life right now. Amen.

Note: You may freely translate the preceding gospel presentation and print it in any form desired. I only ask that no changes be made to it in printed form without written permission. Please bear in mind that it is not intended as a tract to be handed out. Rather, it is a friendship tool for explaining the Good News to your Muslim friend. For this reason, it is best to go through this gradually and prayerfully. Try discussing a new step on each occasion of a meeting with your friend.

Never use this tool hurriedly. The most effective evangelism is persevering, whenever this is possible. This gives time to answer the misconceptions of Muslims, prayerfully preparing them for a heart decision. Most Muslims have spiritual and cultural obstacles that we can never experience. These are considered in later chapters.

For Reflection

1. Which New Testament Gospel is the best to use in dealing with Muslims? Some recommend Matthew for people coming from the occult background of popular Islam. This is partly because Matthew deals much with the Old Testament, where the occult world is laid bare to the truth of God. The genealogy at the beginning speaks volumes to many Muslims, in contrast to the dull unfamiliarity it registers with most Westerners. However, Luke is traditionally the Gospel most recommend, and it certainly is effective for many reasons. I often use the Gospel of John with university students because of its philosophically-oriented concepts coupled with the powerful simplicity of God's truth. Each Gospel has its strong points for use in specific situations.

2. Do I really believe my Muslim friend can accept Christ? We must never suppose that Muslims cannot reach a decision. Muslims do, increasingly, decide for the Lord Jesus. You may well be the instrument God will use to help them. The moment of deci-

sion comes, and when it does, God uses His servants. Read and memorize Romans 10:14–15 and Matthew 11:28.

For Action

1. Examine your methods and your message. Are they pertinent to the felt needs of the friend God has entrusted to your spiritual care, and those of your friend's own circle of friends? The presentation of the gospel in the Word of God varies in style from the literary heights of Isaiah to the impassioned pleas of Peter. The key issue was once expressed by a Moroccan church leader when he told me: "You have to recognize specifically the kind of person to whom you are speaking."

2. How do you see this relationship pattern in the various individuals who decided to follow Christ in John 1? There, brother spoke to brother. Who are your friend's brothers and sisters? Add them to your prayer list.

3. Harm has sometimes been done by "leading a Muslim to Christ" the way we would do it with any person of a Western background. If possible, study the chapters dealing with the Muslim's background before you urge your friend to decide to follow the Lord Jesus. Study the way the four Gospels and Acts lead people to decide for Christ. Our eagerness for a decision may make us run slipshod over cultural and spiritual clues that the Holy Spirit is trying to show us in the life of our friend.

For Additional Study

Among the many excellent books available to help in this area are: *Reaching Muslims For Christ*, by William Saal (Chicago, IL: Moody Press, 1993). Also William McElwee Miller's *A Christian's Response to Islam* (Phillipsburg, NJ: Presbyterian and Reformed Publishing Co., 1980).

3

A Biblical Perspective on Arab Peoples

**Love must be founded on a biblical
understanding. What does
our book, the Bible, say about
your Muslim friend?**

One morning the sun rises, stays in view, and you feel a surge of creativity. You may want to construct something in wood. Perhaps needlepoint or redecoration appeals to you. Whatever the project, there are some basic, initial steps you must take first. You need a plan or pattern to follow in your work. This plan is discovered in prayer to God. He knows both us and our Muslim neighbor. So far in this manual we have explored basic tools; this biblical view of Arabs is our next basic tool.

The afternoon drew to a close in a pleasant little garden behind a small church in the sleepy French town of Castelnaudary. My wife and I had just completed a training session on witnessing to Muslims. I asked Jed, a pastor visiting from the States, if he would like to add a thought. In his soft-spoken way he made the briefest of statements, lengthened only through translation. "I believe the secret of winning Muslims is like winning *anyone* to Christ: they need to see God's love demonstrated in us." These words, spoken in the soft southern sunshine, return to me at times. Love *is* indeed the key. It is a love that will flow from a study and understanding of God's Word.

Later in the book you will see that there is an intense spiritual conflict in winning any Muslim to Christ. The occult world of Islam rages just beneath an outer facade of beautiful buildings and claimed Islamic unity. Chapter Two provided a proven biblical method of presenting Christ to a Muslim. Have you tried it yet? I think you will be surprised with how God can use you. Remember, witness is not just for the experts.

Love and Understanding

I would like to anticipate for a moment a key subject in winning Muslims or anyone else to Christ: love. In Chapter Nine you will see channels along which your love must flow to reach deep into the heart of your God-given Muslim friend. The beauty of love — doesn't this sound like Paul's great anthem of love in 1 Corinthians 13? The seventh principle communicated there is this: **Love must be founded on a biblical understanding.** Your witness must be grounded in the Word of God. Don't Muslims call us the *People of the Book*? What does our book, the Bible, say about your Muslim friend?

Many who use this manual will be working with non-Arab Muslim peoples. You may know a North African Berber, a Pakistani, a Turk or an Indonesian, for example. As a matter of fact, the majority of Muslims are not Arab.[5] But there is a real sense in which your Muslim friend is an Arab inwardly. Any serious Muslim will have been exposed in his mosque and family circle to the Qur'an in the Arabic language. We are the *People of the Book*. As we seek to *be* that, don't we need to consider what the Bible actually says about Arab people?

Charles Malik is the author of *Christ and the University*. He is a former delegate to the United Nations and an Arab Lebanese Christian. In his book, he suggests that the Mideast conflict can never be properly understood without referring to the conflict between Isaac and Ishmael. As you study both Old and New Testaments, you will be a more effective witness. Let's learn how to use the tool of a biblical perspective on Arab peoples.

The form of this chapter will be different from the others. I am going to give you an outline for your own study of Scripture. I hope God will use this to help you to understand a people who have won a real place in my heart. This has only increased through the 30 years I have been getting to know them.

Arabs in the Old Testament

The Beginnings in the Life of Abraham (Genesis 16)

Injustice: Do you feel that Sarah was in any way unjust in her treatment of Hagar? How does this balance with Hagar's own attitude (see verse 4)?[6]

Spirituality: Now read Genesis 16:7–16. Hagar seemed to have more spiritual revelations than her mistress who was chosen by God. She also took them to heart. Do you think this is an overstatement? Can you think of other examples of this in the Genesis story? What does this tell you about the nature of God?

Blessings: To whom were blessings given in verse 10? We will later see that twelve tribes descended from Ishmael, just as they did from Jacob.

Character of Ishmael: Meditate on 16:12. What would be the reaction of your Muslim friend if you read him this passage? What reflections of this do you see in the Arab world today? Why is this not, as it might at first seem, a racist statement (remember the blessings of verse 10 as you answer)? Do you know of some group in your own culture that is characterized by this independence?

The Final Break Between Isaac & Ishmael (Genesis 21)

God Answers: How did God meet Sarah in verses 1–7? Are there any truths or promises here that you can take for your witness and prayer for your Muslim friend? How would you use these in training the young convert God has given you?

The Feast: In verses 8–10, what provoked the schism between the two families? Can you see any application? Read Paul's comments about Ishmael in Galatians 4.

Persecution: Muslims have often persecuted those who follow Jesus Christ as the unique Way to God. Does this account in Genesis help you to deal with this ongoing problem?

Abraham's Love: Does Abraham still love the descendants of his first son (see verse 11)? If, in his lifetime, Abraham still loved his son should we not patiently bear up in prayer even those who reject our message? Isn't it amazing that nearly 4000 years after Abraham lived, God is bringing the descendants of Ishmael to the Messiah? There has never been a time in church history when so many Muslims are turning to the Savior.

The Second Revelation to Hagar: What does Genesis 21:17–18 tell you about the second revelation of the Lord to the mother of the Arabs? What did it mean to her? What provision immediately followed (see verse 19, then 20–21)?

Ishmael's Inheritance: Why do you think that our Father providentially placed so much oil wealth in lands inhabited by Arab and other Muslim peoples? Why did God allow it to lie unused until the 20th century?

The Seeing and Hearing God: God revealed Himself to Hagar as the One who *sees*, then as the One who *hears*. In what ways has God seen the suffering of Muslim peoples today? Is the unprecedented   Christian   outreach   to   them   an   example?

The Twelve Tribal Leaders of Ishmael

Figure 4: The Sons of Ishmael (Genesis 25:13-16)

Ishmael's Generations (Genesis 25:12–18)

God's Blessing: What does this passage tell you about God's blessing on Ishmael? How is this reflected in the number of tribes descended from him?

Ishmael's Descendants: Note the names of these tribes. Historically, what has been their position regarding those who follow the Bible? Do you see any significance to our situation today? Do you pray for any of these nations or their equivalents? For help with your answer, note the mention of Egypt (25:12) and Shur (25:18); Shur is on Egypt's northeast border.

Now you can begin to see how important it is to understand God's Old Testament revelation about the Arabs. I remember enjoying a cartoon by Lawing in *Christianity Today*. It depicted two Hebrews discussing Ishmael. They said that they shouldn't worry about Ishmael, since "our descendants will probably never run into one another." In fact, the Old Testament stories are a key to understanding so many of the complications that have arisen when their descendants *did* run into one another.

I am reminded of Wendy Stanford, who faithfully served Christ in Montpellier with a youth team. She told me how she had been blessed by the example of a young North African Christian's patience in suffering. We may learn many lessons from our Arab friends, Christian and non-Christian alike. We should remember that the roots of their experience are right here in this book of beginnings.[7]

Arabs in the New Testament

Matthew 27:32

Who was compelled to carry the cross of Christ? From what country did he come? Look this up in a Bible dictionary to find his origins. Note, however, that he was not an Arab but a Hellenistic Jew.

Acts 2:10–11

What is the positioning of Arabs in this list? Do you see any significance here? Who do you think they were? Check a commentary for additional insight.

Galatians 4:21–31

Freedom Versus Slavery: How does this apply to Christian versus Islamic beliefs? How would your belief affect dealings with your Muslim friend?

Flesh Versus Promise: How would this help you in evaluating the idea that *zeal for religion* means a person is pious and wins favor with God?

How do these truths show us the confrontational nature of the Christian message and its conflict with any other human sect or religion?

Are you beginning to see the importance of these essential facts in Scripture? They can prepare us for understanding the Arab and Muslim world. Do you see how these truths can help us understand our Muslim friends? Pierre Jox, formerly Minister of the Interior in France, had some advice during a crisis in the Mideast. He said: *"Ne paniquons pas!"* ("Let's not panic!") How can we avoid panic in communicating God's love? Calm comes when our roots go deep into the Word of God and we build our relationships on biblical foundations.

Some Applications

There are two parts to God's answer, each with its own particular context and insight. First comes the Old, and only then the New Testament. St. Augustine's famous statement is very apropos here: "The New is in the Old concealed; the Old is in the New revealed."

The Church and Israel

People often say, "Israel is the People of God." They may use this as a cover-up for a negative attitude toward all Arabs. I believe that Romans 9–11 teaches that Israel is not the People of God in this era. One day they will be grafted in (Romans 11:17–24) and again take a key place in God's plan. The People of God today are French, Norwegians, Americans, Algerians, Jordanians: any and all who truly have received Christ. This has been true since the church was first established on the foundation of the Jewish people.

The 20th-century church includes Jews. Evangelical Palestinians, however, outnumber Jewish believers in Israel today. Still, Paul tells us "all Israel will be saved" in the day of Christ's return. Two facts are clear from these passages. First, Christians have differing positions on this knotty question. Second, we need to understand what the whole Bible teaches in order to witness effectively among Muslims.

The True Conflict in the Middle East

On the very day of a major conflict in the Mideast, our little team in Toulouse had unknowingly scheduled an extended prayer meeting. This reminded me that the true warfare for Christians was not the Crusades of the Middle Ages. Nor is spiritual warfare some contemporary armed conflict. Our warfare is to put on the whole armor of God and to intercede. Paul reminds us of this in Ephesians 6. Are we overly influenced by what we hear and see in the media? We need the realism of what God tells us in the Bible. Then we become, in our personal experience, what our Muslim friends call us: the *People of the Book*. We become soldiers on the *spiritual front line* as we personally intercede for the Muslim world.

Beware of Syncretism

Syncretism is the combining of elements from two or more religions, trying to bring out the best of both. How do Muslims survive in our pluralistic Western countries? Most try to live and let live when it comes to their religious practice. Their solution, therefore, is that Jesus is one of many ways to God. They may even pray to accept Christ. Yet, in their hearts, they may still evade Christ's uniqueness. For this reason we must make the choice very clear. *Christ did!* Jesus said that He was *the* way, not just *a* way. He is the Prophet of God, Priest and King. Jesus Christ is not just a prophet among others. He is not only the son of Miriam (Mary), as the Qur'an identifies Him, He is the unique Son of God. Beware of decisions that come quickly and easily. It is only as we stay in the Bible that we keep our focus on the narrowness of God's truth.

Focus on the Key Question: "Where Do I Find Eternal Life?"

The Bible is quite clear in John 17:3: "Now this is eternal life: that they may know you, the only true God, and Jesus Christ, whom you have sent." Many Muslims are quite gifted in conversation and enjoy a good debate. We need to keep the focus always on the simple, mighty message of life in the Son.

The "Wisest" Can Be the Most Foolish

When I worked at university bookstands, I learned how many knowledgeable students had little knowledge when it came to the vital subject of God. Many Muslims receive religious teaching in childhood. But I found that many have forgotten or lost interest in the subject of God. This barrier can cause us dismay. Neither should we be intimidated by powerful arguments from the more zealous Muslims. Paul tells us in the first chapters of 1 Corinthians that God's wisdom and man's wisdom are at two different poles. Knowing the background of Arabs from Scripture helps us to approach them on their own turf. Our message becomes meaningful and relevant to them.

Help From One Who Has Been There

A good friend, Abdullah, grew up in a nominal Muslim home in France. Now a Christian, he once gave a conference for pastors of the French Free Churches on communicating Christ to Muslims. Abdullah himself moved from skepticism to a deep love for the Lord. He keeps that faith in spite of some very trying events in his personal life. I would like to include elements of the seminar here to help you see his unique perspective.

Understanding Islam Biblically

Hebrews 9:22 teaches that without the shedding of blood there is no forgiveness. Also Numbers 19:9 and its context speaks of the ritual of the red heifer, illustrating the same truth in a context familiar to many Muslims. The story of the instituting of the Passover in Exodus 12 also speaks of this.

Another parallel passage is Genesis 22, the story of Isaac and the sacrifice. Abdullah says: "All Muslims know this story. We can point out to them that all believers in the Old Testament come to God by means of sacrifice" (cf. Hebrews 10:1–8, 12).

Pictures of the Cross

- **The brass serpent** lifted up (John 3:14). Show your Muslim friend that in the same way *Jesus* was lifted up on the cross for the sins of people. This shows that God is sovereign in this wonderful act. As we preach God's Word, we should lift up Jesus, just as Moses did the serpent.

- **The Good Shepherd**, who gives His life for the sheep (John 10; 12:24). He is also the one Mediator between God and man (1 Timothy 2:4–5). Abdullah adds: "If two people have an argument, they need a mediator, a third person, to reconcile them." This is a picture that is very familiar in Islamic culture. We should underline the fact that people must be reconciled with *God*, and not the other way around. Ask your friend for examples of this in his own family experience.

Texts for Use in Witness

- Romans 3:22–23 "For there is no difference, for all have sinned and fall short of the glory of God."

- Romans 6:23 "For the wages of sin is death, but the gift of God is eternal life in Christ Jesus our Lord."

- Ephesians 2:8 "For it is by grace you have been saved, through faith — and this not from yourselves, it is the gift of God..."

- 1 Timothy 2:3–4 "God our Savior, who wants all men to be saved and to come to a knowledge of the truth."

- Hebrews 9:22 "...Without the shedding of blood there is no forgiveness."

A Parting Thought

Finally, Abdullah emphasizes that without being convinced of sin, a person will never seek after a Savior. Muslims will never truly repent until they see that sin is really a revolt against God. Submission to Christ as Lord will never come if the Holy Spirit doesn't convict your friend. Therefore we are absolutely dependent on the Holy Spirit. Pray often that the Spirit will convict your Muslim friends of *their sin*.

Conclusion

We have looked quickly at scriptures in both Old and New Testaments that concern the history and character of the Arab peoples. As you study, you will be a more effective witness. You followed the blueprint, measured and estimated. You have labored long and hard to cut your piece or set up your creative project. You are now ready for the final inspection. Acquiring a biblical perspective is like that final inspection.

Of course your study and experience of the Bible should continue as an integral part of your follow-up. It may be along the lines of suggestions mentioned above, or you may continue by following your own track. After all, aren't you working with the very choice *material* of a man or woman from the Muslim world, made in the image of God?

For Action

1. Write out an approach you could use with a Muslim from these passages in Genesis.

2. How would a Bible study from these passages help young Muslim converts to be stronger in living in their family circle?

3. My wife often likens the suffering of Hagar to that of Muslim women with whom she works today. How can you use the Hagar story as a bridge to a Muslim woman you know?

For Additional Study

1. Take a concordance, note and then write out summaries of all the entries under the word "Arab." Also look up "Ishmaelites." Check these terms in a Bible dictionary. Seek to discover the relation of this people to other Semitic peoples in the Bible.

2. Review the beliefs of Islam in a book like *Reaching Muslims for Christ*. How are the roots we discover in the Bible reflected in present Islamic practices? Build a chart showing your thoughts, putting "Practice" and "Bible passage" in parallel columns.

3. Read a book on church history to discover the role of North Africans in the development of the early church. What particular biblical issues did St. Augustine bring into our faith? Remember that Augustine was a Berber convert to Christianity from paganism in AD 386. How would his example speak to Berber peoples of North Africa today? Note that no other author so greatly influenced John Calvin, the French Reformation founder and theologian.

4

Answering Muslim Questions

**Often we pay too much attention
to the fervent argument of our Muslim friend.
We should be praying and aiming for
the real heart need.**

My wife and I greatly enjoy participating in the youth teams of Operation Mobilization. Team members, with little if any experience, often find that Muslim young people are ready to listen to them. A typical day begins with men and women singing heartily all together. Slowly the cobwebs caused by lack of sleep begin to disappear. Then the team spends a significant and unforgettable time in studying the Bible. This is coupled with intense times of seeking God in prayer for themselves and for those they will speak with throughout the day.

The Bible often teaches about prayer. It also has much teaching about itself — its inspiration, authority, and interpretation, for example. The Bible doctrines of prayer and Scripture are closely linked. We have considered the importance of prayer in presenting the gospel to your Muslim neighbor. *Five Steps on the*

Straight Path (see pages 28–29) helped us put feet to our prayers. But how do we interpret Scripture to a Muslim? The Steps helped, as did our study of Arabs in the Bible. We also need to discover biblical insight into the specific heart need of our friend. A good summary of our preparation would be: *Pray! Speak! Study!*

The next tool in our box also concerns Scripture. An important question may have been lurking in the back of your mind: "What about these issues my friend raises, like Christ's deity, or His death on the cross? Are we simply to ignore them, assuming that they are a smoke screen?" Often this *is* the case, as Muslims try to remove the heat of God's convicting Word from their consciences.

Answering Objections

Figure 5: What the Muslim Believes and Feels

My first suggestion is to avoid dealing with most questions right away. My second, however, is to deal with them eventually. A number of excellent books contain answers in varied detail to common questions posed by Muslims. It is not necessary in a manual like this to go over the same ground in detail. Our purpose is to provide you with tools to work with Muslims in Western countries. It is useful to provide you with an outline of the most common objections. We do need to remember a vital point: there is probably a marked difference between what our Muslim friends say and what they actually think.

An Arab proverb is familiar to us: "If words were of silver, then silence would be of gold." Often we pay too much attention to the fervent argument of our Muslim friend. **We should be praying and aiming for the real heart need.** A Muslim once launched into an argument with an Arab Christian leader. Then the leader began speaking of man's universal need of heart peace. Immediately the Muslim changed his tune. "I'm so glad you said that," he replied. "I felt I had to defend Islam, so I spoke first defending my faith. You are right — I do need peace." The Christian went on to explain the gospel to a very receptive listener.

As I pointed out in our chapter on the Gospel Presentation, however, there is a time to answer their objections. There is an important reason for this.[8] Professor Jean Bichon, then at the University of Algiers, spoke at a seminar on Islam and Christianity at the Protestant Church in Rabat, Morocco. Suddenly, he pronounced these stunning words: "Islam denies the very heart of what we believe." His words echoed out powerfully in the old Protestant Church. Some of the more liberal Protestants in attendance expressed pained shock. He was, nevertheless, right on target. Many obstacles are scattered across the path of our dialogue and witness. There is a place, therefore, for answers at these points of conflict.

We have the example of our Lord Jesus in His debates with the Pharisees and Sadducees in Matthew 22:15–46. He ended with a

biblical proof of His divinity as the Son of God. His words profoundly upset His ardent but confused monotheistic listeners.
Muslims are shocked with the tenets of our faith for some of the
same reasons. We need to help them believe in Him who is the
way, the truth and the life. We must answer their objections. Jesus answered questions and so should we!

Common Objections
The Bible has been changed or corrupted.
How can you say that God has a son?
Why is it that you never speak about the Prophet Muhammed?
Christ did not die as Christians claim he did.

Table 1: Common Objections (in approximate order of frequency encountered)

Various other objections are also used. For example: The Trinity
cannot be true. Why do Christians eat pork or drink alcohol? Why
don't they keep the Ramadan fast month? Some also raise objections which come from their secular or political orientation.

The Bible Has Been Changed

Let me begin with a warning: Don't be like Pilgrim, in John Bun-
yan's *Pilgrim's Progress*, who was led along a bypass and into a
meadow of wandering. He nearly fell off a cliff and joined the
broken bodies below. Our battle with the Muslim is not a battle of
the Books but a battle of Persons. Is it Christ or Muhammed who
is the way to God? Avoid being drawn into a heated argument.

Ask your friend: "You claim it has been changed. Tell me, then,
who changed it, and at what time and place in history? What texts

in the Bible have been changed?" Then ask: "Was it changed *before* or *after* your prophet Muhammed?"

If it was *before Muhammed*, then why does the Qur'an praise the Bible and commend its reading (cf. Surah 2:130). If it was *after Muhammed*, there are many manuscripts and other sources for determining the Bible's authenticity.[9]

The Qur'anic Witness

The Qur'an does *not* really say that the Bible was changed. The Qur'an *does* say that the Qur'an itself has been changed (cf. Surahs 2:100; 22:51). The *tawraat, zabuur* and *injiil* are all referred to in the Qur'an without criticism. Why would it do so if the Qur'an taught that the Bible had been changed?

External Evidence

There is much external evidence to demonstrate that the Bible was not changed. Some of these evidences are:

- Ancient translations of the Bible
- Bible quotations in early Christian writers
- Self-contradictions of Bible critics. I like to use the example of Bishop Robinson who changed his mind about the alleged errors in John's Gospel after examining the evidence.[10]
- Archeological evidence. Johns Hopkins University scholar William Foxwell Albright was one of the most outstanding archeologists of his time. He gradually shifted from unquestioning acceptance of higher critical views of Scripture to accepting the Bible at its face value.

Modern Skeptics

Maurice Bucaille is a contemporary author widely quoted by Muslims in Europe and elsewhere. He rejects the Bible's claim to be the Word of God, primarily by alleged scientific and historical inaccuracies. For a more detailed examination of his arguments, see *The Qur'an and the Bible in the Light of History and Science* by Dr. William Campbell.

Jesus Is Not the Son of God

The Meaning of the Term

A few days before writing this chapter, I spoke for a long time with a militant Muslim. His brow knitted in a troubled expression, he questioned how God could have a son. At first, this very intense older Moroccan man had listened to my presentation of the gospel. (Remember to present the gospel first, if at all possible; then deal with problems.) So I began to answer him by first returning to his question:

> "Tell me what *you* understand we believe when we speak of Jesus as the Son of God." My friend stated somewhat triumphantly: "Well, do you believe God had a family?" Obviously I did not, so grasping his hand I said, "Absolutely not! I don't believe that any more than you do. Now we agree. Now let me tell you what 'Son of God' does mean. Your Qur'an uses the term 'son of the road' for a traveler. Does this mean the road was married and had a child? Of course not! The meaning is not a physical one. The traveler is thought of as taking on the *nature of the road*, so he becomes its son, so to speak. The son, in a figurative sense, has *the nature of his father*."

I went on to explain that this is how it is with Jesus as the Son of God. Jesus forgave sins. Only God can do this. Therefore Jesus is the Son of God. This usually leads to the story of Jesus and the paralyzed man. Like many stories, it can grip the attention of your Muslim friend at a moment when he might feel quite combative.

The Story of the Four Friends and Jesus

Read Matthew 9:1–8 and its parallels in other Gospels. This is my favorite story for demonstrating the deity of our Lord Jesus. Tell how Jesus announced to the paralyzed man that his sins were forgiven. Then stress the unbelief of the religious leaders. They angrily challenged Jesus Christ.

Your friend may well see a parallel with Islam. Some people who profess to be very religious can actually be strongly opposed to the teaching of God about His Son. Jesus forgave the paralytic. This meant that Jesus was indeed the Son of God. He possessed God's own nature. *Who can forgive sins, except God alone?*

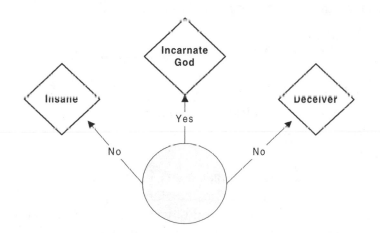

Figure 6: Who is Jesus?

Another approach I use is to ask, "Have you read the Bible? No? Well, you must, because until you do you cannot understand this very important question." Ask the Muslim to read a passage of Scripture, such as the above story. Try to set a meeting time for the next week. You may ask on that occasion if your friend has a particularly meaningful passage for you to read in the Qur'an. Most don't respond to this. Those that do may say something like: "You should read the whole Qur'an." Here it is important to be able to say that you have read some of it. I would recommend that you read the first Surah (chapter), and also the second, the Surah of Miriam.

Focus on the Character of Jesus

It is vitally important here to focus the discussion on Christ Himself. To do this, you might ask a summary question: "Did you notice that Jesus Himself taught that He was the Son of God? Look here in Matthew 16:13–20." I might also turn to the "I am" passages of John's Gospel (e.g., John 14:6). "In saying this, was Jesus insane? Was He deliberately deceiving His listeners? Or was He, in fact, the Son of God as He Himself stated?"

Jesus Did Not Die on the Cross

The Purpose of the Cross

Explain to your Muslim friend the *goal* of Jesus' death, according to the Bible. Your friend probably sees it as a defeat. We see it as a great victory.

Turn to John 1:29. It says that Jesus is the Lamb of God. His cousin, that great prophet John the Baptizer, says so. Then you can go from the known to the unknown, by speaking of the Muslims' greatest festival day. This is *al-'iid al-aDHa*, also called the Sheep Feast or *al-'iid al-kabiir*. The devout Muslim buys a sheep for his family and offers it in memory of Abraham's sacrifice. Muslims also often see in this a means to atone for sins. Explain how Jesus on the cross said "It is finished" (*tetelestai*, all is fully accomplished)!

You can then explain the sacrifice of Abraham, from Genesis 22. Show how this is a picture of the death of God's only Son. In the same way, Abraham was prepared to offer his only son according to God's covenant promise. It is good to go on to say that this is why we do not offer sacrifices today. Muslims do, at the time of the Sheep Feast. The sacrifice was a picture of Christ. This picture was fulfilled when He came, so it is now abolished. We have nothing left to do, except to believe God's promise and to obey His Word.

Predictions about the Cross

Point out that Christ's death was predicted many times in the Bible. Read Isaiah 52:13–53:12. Perhaps this passage has specially touched you, or someone else you know. Show how the Messiah, Christ, loved us enough to die for us. Explain how this transformed your own life. You may also like to share the Messianic Psalms (e.g., 22, 23, and 24). Remember the use of prophecy, with the historic time line illustration (cf. p. 35).

As in the discussion about Jesus as Son of God, ask your friend what was Jesus' own testimony about Himself and His death? Matthew 20:28 is a good verse to use. Even better, read whole passages from the Gospels on Jesus' death. You may also use Matthew 16:13–23. Jesus' death is made clear here by a statement from His own lips. This is also useful for showing Jesus' Sonship. Have you noticed that Jesus' Sonship and His death are often joined in Scripture, as here in Matthew?

The Centrality of the Cross

Show your friend the large amount of space given to Jesus' death by each Gospel writer. In the case of John, almost half of his Gospel speaks of Jesus' death and resurrection. In all of the Gospels, there is much more on Jesus' death than on His virgin birth (accepted by Muslims, while His death is rejected). His death is dealt with more than any other event in His life. You may want actually to turn to one Gospel with your friend and demonstrate this, holding the pertinent pages in your hand.

The Cross and the Resurrection

The final proof of Jesus' death and its meaning is in the resurrection. "It is true! The Lord has risen." Read 1 Corinthians 15 with your friend. Or you might compare Luke 1:1–3 with Luke 24. You could use the Emmaus Road story here, as it would appeal to the Eastern mind and culture.

You may be asking yourself: "How can I read scripture on Jesus' death to a Muslim when Islam rejects the very fact itself?" Your Muslim neighbor may not believe that Jesus really died. Yet this in no way prevents God from working. Saul was full of anger and bent on tormenting Christians. This didn't keep God's Word from stopping him abruptly on the road to Damascus (cf. Acts 9). He never forgot this experience with Christ, retelling it three times in the book of Acts.

Bear in mind an underlying problem: Muslims believe that death is a defeat, and that God does not let His prophets suffer ultimate defeat. Remind your friend that Muhammad, whom Muslims believe was a prophet, also suffered greatly. Some say he even died from the poison of one of his wives, a Jewess. Be that as it may, many true prophets suffer. You can tell the story of Job (*siidna ayuub*) as a prime example. You can then remind the Muslim that for Jesus it was a victory, not a defeat.

Your Personal Witness

Use your own testimony. How did you come to realize that Jesus had died for you? What verses struck you? Use them with your friend. A personal knowledge of God speaks volumes to many who have seen too much of materialistic Westerners. Share how you are different now that Christ has entered your life. Remember Revelation 12:11: "They overcame him [Satan] by the blood of the Lamb and by the word of their testimony; and they did not love their lives so much as to shrink from death."

The Trinity Is Impossible

It is best not to go very far in this subject, as the unconverted heart cannot understand the things of God. Keep in mind always that by "Trinity" Muslims always understand three gods (father mother, son). We always need, therefore, to remind them "you are in error because you do not know the Scriptures or the power of God" (Matthew 22:29). Kundan Massey suggests that the Trinity is not, as many assume, like *addition*; we should think instead of *multiplication*. Consider the formula: 1+1+1=3. Then change it to: 1x1x1=1. The result is still one. It is helpful to point out that Islam believes that *allaahu akbar*, God is all powerful. How, then, should we expect to have a simple answer on the question of His infinite Being?

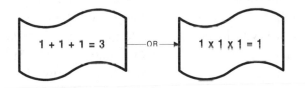

Figure 7: Confusion about the Trinity

One excellent tool for an interested Muslim is the story of *abuu yuusef*. This is on a half-hour video cassette, and is especially powerful because the North African brother involved shares his testimony right from the area in North Africa where he grew up. He points out that he is the father of his child, the child of his own father, and the husband of his wife. These three relations don't mean he is three persons. He is one person, just as God is three persons in one essence. Deuteronomy 6:4, along with Jesus' quotations of it, is very useful. I add 1 Timothy 2:5: "*one* God, *one* mediator between God and men." Speak of this at the proper time. Be careful, however, not to throw your pearls before swine.

Also explain to your friend that finite human illustrations can never adequately explain God's spiritual reality.

Islam Is the Ideal Political System

Religious or Secular?

There are two categories of politically-oriented Muslims. The first have a calmer Islamic penetration of society in mind. They want to form neighborhood associations that will effect religious, social and political change. The second group is the Islamic Fundamentalists. Are they not the most religious of all, enforcing a strict relationship to Allah? While they may quote the Qur'an, many I have talked to seem to know only a limited amount of its contents. Uppermost in the fundamentalist's mind is a Machiavellian manipulation of society. They would impose an Islamic structure in a given locality by force. That structure is their own version of Islam, which differs from many others. At heart, they also are political and therefore secularist. How do we answer these two types of secularists?

Christians Are People of Integrity

Yasmina lived in a popular quarter in a large Muslim city. When a problem with the law arose, the police would often come to her. They knew she was a Christian and that she would tell the truth, even if no one else did.

Muslims can be guilty of manipulation. You can tell your friend that Muslims use material incentives to encourage conversion to Islam. One student I knew was a fervent member of a Muslim organization on campus. I saw him offer money to help a Muslim friend to whom I was witnessing. The message was clear: "Stick with us, and we'll see you have enough to live on." An Egyptian in one American university town told me how he visited a mosque. They thought he was a Muslim, and encouraged him to find an American wife in order to further Islam. Are these methods spiritual or God-honoring in any sense?

Politicized Muslims think that the political system of Islam is superior to all others. You may want to point out that *if* it is so, why is there persecution of Christians in Muslim countries? Does God need help in establishing His Islamic society? The wife of a fine North African believer was pregnant. She was interrogated by the police, then taken outside of town. The authorities then left her to walk the long distance home after dark. What crime had she committed against her State that merited this brutal treatment? A foreign Christian doctor, much loved and needed in his community, was expelled with his wife from a Muslim country. A pastor and his wife in another country were escorted in a police car to the airport. The police officer was upset that the lady was crying. He asked her why. She tearfully replied that they were being forced out of the land they lived in for twenty years. Years of sacrificial love and good relations between Muslims and Christians suddenly went up in smoke.

Responsible Citizenship and Social Change

Talk to your Muslim friend of the example of Jesus Christ. Jesus told Peter to put away his sword. Muhammed, on the other hand, actively encouraged and led Jihad or Holy War. As soon as possible, however, attempt to turn the conversation to God's power to change hearts. Change in society often follows, as history demonstrates. Share what this change meant in your own situation.

With students, you can tell of the Wesleys in England. They transformed the terribly corrupt 18th-century society to an extent that even some secular historians recognize. Their "weapons" were popular hymns and sermons delivered in unlikely places, like cemeteries. The people, small and great, flocked to hear them. What political program could ever accomplish change that profound?

Alain Choiquier is a prominent French evangelist of Algerian origin. He tells the story of a Marxist student he met years ago. The young Marxist was ranting about how Communism would radically transform society. Choiquier replied: "Tell me, have you seen any change?" "No, but we're moving towards it," replied the Communist. Then the evangelist said: "But we Christians have *already* experienced change. We are new persons in Christ (2 Corinthians 5:17)." Then he went on to explain the gospel to a ready listener, who later accepted the Lord.

It is good, when possible, to close a discussion like this one with the subject of the power of prayer to change warped lives. Tell your secular or Islamic friend how you talk with God, how God has answered you. Explain how, through prayer, you are changing your world. Ask if your friend has talked with God or feels close to Him. Mention that you are praying for your friend's personal needs and relationship with God.

A Final Word

Some thinking Muslims like to ask what they believe to be an unanswerable question. They bring together two seemingly contradictory Qur'anic teachings. The first is "God is the most terrible of those who punish" (*shadiid al-'iqaab*); the second is that God is "the pardoning and merciful One" (*al-ghafuur, ar-raHiim*). "How can both be true?" they say. "Yet we are obligated to accept them." Both of these, God's mercy and God's wrath, are also great Bible emphases in the plan of God. In Islam, the only way to reconcile these two opposite poles is our good works. In this way, Muslims seek shelter and salvation from the wrath to come. *Human* actions bring the mercy of God to us. Grace does not exist.

The Bible, however, brings us another conclusion. Jesus Christ, as the God-Man, has come between mercy and wrath. At the cross, He took God's wrath on Himself, as our substitute. So in Him alone we find forgiveness.

One evening I was discussing this question with a group of committed Christian university students. I asked them, "What comes between these two truths to join them?" One answered, "God's justice." This is just what the Apostle Paul says in Romans 3:26. Paul spoke of how to appropriate the sacrifice of Christ's atonement. He then explained that God does this "so as to be just and the One who justifies those who have faith in Jesus." What is the relationship between God's mercy and God's wrath? Christians have discovered the answer while Muslims remain troubled by the question. They have no satisfying answer. You can see the basic conflict behind many outward questions the Muslim poses. We should seek to touch this raw nerve of personal need with the good news of forgiveness. As we do this, we present the answer which has always escaped the thinking of our Muslim friend.

Why *do* Muslims pose all those questions? Because they struggle with unbelief. The Gospel of John has been called the Gospel of Belief. Yet as you study its pages, you see that it is also the Gospel of *unbelief*! The process of rejection of Jesus by the religious leaders is clearly outlined as the story goes forward. This unbelief grows downward, toward the pit. All the while, the belief of the disciples grows upward toward the Father in heaven. How can you convince your doubting Muslim friend? Pray that the friend will be like Thomas, and cry out "My Lord, and my God."

Nathaniel at first despised Christ, asking if anything good could come out of Nazareth (John 1:46). Yet he ended up a disciple. Doubting Nathaniel drilled the foundations of his spiritual house into the bedrock of the Son of David, the Son of God. Muslims all over the world are overcoming their unbelief. Remember the central place of prayer? Trust God to bring your friend into the community of belief, as a member of the family of faith.

For Additional Study

Study the excellent works that deal with Muslim objections. One previously referred to is *Reaching Muslims for Christ*, by William J. Saal. The writings of Charles Marsh are also most helpful. Take time to do further Bible study on any key question that seems to be troubling your Muslim friend. Select a question that comes up often, but recognize that it may be a smoke screen. Concentrate prayer on finding how to hit at the spiritual root of the problem.[11]

5

Understanding Muslim Culture

**Friendship is the key to penetration.
Outsiders are treated with great respect
if they are brought into the family circle.**

I opened a mysterious envelope one day to discover that it contained a worn piece of paper in the older Arabic, Qur'anic style of script. It was identifiable as a magic charm by its form, writing and vocabulary. I wondered why it had come from a North African Christian friend. He had not thought to send me any explanation. Months later I learned that he and his wife had found this under their bed. He asked me: "Do you think this was intended for good or for evil?" He wondered if the sender employed white or black magic. He was sure that his parents had placed it there.

When I explained that it was designed to break up their marriage, the gap that separated them from their parents widened. The loving prayer burden these children had for their parents continued, however. Years later they had opportunities to fulfill the command in Exodus 20:12: "Honor your father and your mother." In the midst of the parents' sickness and marital problems, their own marriage became a powerful testimony of faithfulness and love. I saw again how Muslim culture is hard to fathom — at times even for them.

In any building project, the builder searches the toolbox for the appropriate tools. Prayer and proclamation of the gospel go hand in hand. We seek to know our Muslim friend better by studying what the Bible says about Arab peoples. Pointed questions lead us to prayerful, biblical answers. When our Muslim friend understands Christ's dying love, then we use our finishing tools.

In this chapter we will consider the tool of knowing our Muslim neighbors. They come from a setting very different from our own. We need to examine this world as we spend time with them. We should prayerfully ask God to help us find the way into their hearts. This is similar to the carpenter knowing his building materials. The unique talents and culture of our friend are much more valuable than we first think. Bricks, mortar, rough wood, or a ball of unworked yarn may seem nearly valueless. As we work with them, however, we find out what they can become. We then appreciate them for what they are, discovering their intrinsic value.

Study people and observe them carefully at home and in the marketplace. You will find your witness more pointed. You may also discover deepening acceptance among your friend's family and friends. Christians who witness to their Muslim neighbors should be involved in an informal type of research. Jesus initiated a *theological* discussion with Nicodemus (John 3), but a *practical* one with the woman at the well (John 4). Our Lord knew them both intimately. Prayerfully study the world of your friend.

Most of us come from a more Western-oriented, individualistic culture. Muslims, even in Western countries, are usually part of a complex, interrelated family structure. This structure is probably quite different from our own. It may even extend across continents and oceans to the original land of a Muslim's family. How can an understanding of their families help us win them to Christ?

The sensitive evangelist may find a deep sense of loyalty in the Muslim. This may begin with the family and extend out into the neighborhood and the country of origin. It also probably touches their ethnic people-grouping (e.g., Algerian, Lebanese, Pakistani, or Berber). The family chain may become a channel for the gospel.

Family unity can play an important role. An Eastern proverb illustrates this: "Me against my brother, my brother and I against my cousin, all of us against the foreigner." When the Arabs in an area are singled out for abuse, they may band together. A striking example of this was a march from Marseille to Paris in 1983. This political pilgrimage ended in an interview with the President of France, François Mitterand. In this case the larger group loyalty bonded them for action. What are your friend's loyalties? How may these become avenues for making Christ known?

Said's family lives more or less apart from his parents. They treated his wife as a servant girl when she lived in their home (a practice not uncommon in North Africa and often brought over to France). The family's goal was to divide the son from his wife so that his first loyalty would be to them. It was only with great difficulty that Said preserved his marriage. God eventually used him to win his wife to his Savior.

Family loyalties may be seen by younger Muslims as an albatross around their necks. They often will seek to break free from them. At the same time, they well realize the need for their extended families. For believers, Jesus' instructions about family opposition usually become dramatically real. Our Lord said: "Brother will betray brother to death, and a father his child; children will rebel against their parents and have them put to death. All men will hate you because of me" (Matthew 10:21–23). (See also Matthew 10:34–38 and 19:29).

Group relationships are a vital concern for the *second genera-tion*.[12] This is traceable in part to their Islamic concept of *umma* (community). The foundational relationship is their extended family. Other relationships generally follow this one. Your rela-tionship with your Muslim friend may well start gospel truth flowing down the lines of existing family relations.

Understanding the Muslim Family

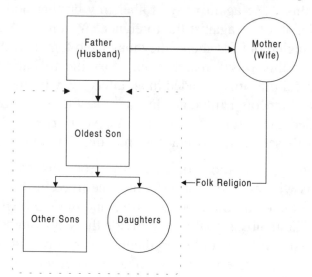

Figure 8: Family Dynamics

Let me sum up. Young Muslims in the West experience deep ties with their peer group. Their cultural ties, however, flow most strongly from their immediate family. For this reason, we need to understand more fully our friend's family structure. One North African friend is the oldest brother in his family. He asserts: "In our family milieu, those who have the most authority are the father, over the mother and the children, and the oldest son over the sisters." A second friend adds: "The father gives the orders. The mother can't even suggest an idea. This is changing, but only thanks to European influence." A third, a former university student, enlarges on this: "The father has the place of authority, as well as the grandfather, if he is living, or the grandmother." The family structure that I often encounter in my own work may help you to understand that of your Muslim friend.

The Father

The father is theoretically at the apex of the triangle of family relations. In Arab families, he is the titular head of the home. All family decisions must pass through him. This is, of course, very similar to Jewish culture in the Bible.

In Matthew 1, for example, the men are the ones through whom the family is linked. Notice that there is reference to only four women in addition to Mary: Tamar, Rahab, Ruth, and Bathsheba. I found this principle duplicated when working with the Mohlim family. I visited the father and befriended him. One day he said: "I don't care where my children go when they are with Monsieur Jean (his title of respect for me); I have confidence in him." The only exception to this rule of authority is when the father is unable to function in this role. Here the eldest son or one of his brothers may take charge.

The Oldest Son

The oldest son takes over the discipline of all siblings. For example, consider the harsh role performed by Mahmoud, typical of more traditional North African families. Mahmoud was a terrible taskmaster as *"l'aîné de la famille"* (the firstborn). When he came to know Christ, however, he became much closer to his sister. In the past, it had been his responsibility to beat her. She was amazed to see his gentleness and change of attitude toward her. He continued to hold his former position as family head, yet now he sought the good of others and not just the brutal exercise of his prerogatives. This was a major factor in his sister later accepting Christ.

The Mother

The mother, however, often exerts a great deal of influence on the children since she is with them much of the time. Her role is usually most enduring for the children since she is the one who passes on the group's religious values. This includes not only traditional Islam but also knowledge of the occult. In Matthew 1, we can also see how God broke with Jewish tradition: God inspired Matthew's genealogy so that it stressed His grace operating in the lives of women. They are often key figures in His plan of love and mercy. Jesus' first resurrection appearance was to a woman. The gospel cleanses and conditions a mother's love. This can transform a Muslim home.

Other Family Members

Older family members are generally respected, at least to their faces. We can learn much from our Arab friends in this. Male members of the society often have many advantages over female members. With the onset of puberty, girls often stay at home after school to work in the house. This is designed, in part, to keep them pure until marriage. Boys, on the other hand, may roam at will from a young age. I find something admirable about these independent, free-wheeling young people. They develop a very particular mindset that helps them cope with the many stresses of living. One of the greatest traits is an ability to cope with life at what many consider to be a lower rung of the social ladder.

Other Relations

As mentioned above, the boys give orders to the girls. An older male relative can replace the father in taking charge of the women. Turia was terribly afraid of her uncle. Not only did he serve as a family authority figure, he was also deeply involved with occult practices.

Relations apart from the family are very loose in the *second generation*. Friends will include both Western peers and other Muslims. For women, however, friendships are more limited. This is true in spite of the constant evolution of social status for younger women. The first generation is passing off the scene. Younger women's lives, however, are still usually colored by the traditional Muslim home. Its focus is on raising children and the extended family obligations.

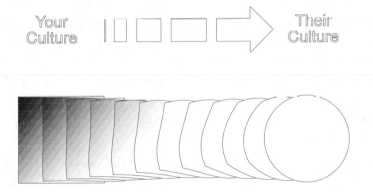

Figure 9: Cultural Transformation

The female work ethic touches this group. Many young women dream of moving out of the home and into their own apartments, with their own jobs. In many Muslim homes, a wife will not relate much to her in-laws. This is because of the magnetic pull of her husband's parent's desire to bring their son under their authority. Young women are not as accessible for fellowship as are young men, although this too is changing with time. Men, on the other hand, will bring outsiders much more freely into the friendship circle. These may come from work, the neighborhood, school, or the local bar or youth club. Non-Muslims are often numbered among the friends of young Muslim singles and couples. All of these observations vary according to nationality, the parents' mentality, and several other factors.

Remember that we often fail to understand that our own culture has a very different shape than that of our Muslim friend. Ours could be thought of as square, the Muslim's as round. We need to ask the Spirit of God for understanding of these differences. Then God will help us to round off some of our cultural angles so that we may better love our friend for Jesus' sake.

Friendship is a two-way street. One striking example was an anti-racist campaign in France. It's slogan declared: *"Touche pas mon pôte!"* ("Hands off my pal!"). Both French and Arab Muslims joined in this campaign, the French standing up for their North African friends. This went as far as interviews by high government officials with these pioneering young people. Outsiders became insiders as French and Arab youths worked together. Examples like this help us to determine how we can gain the confidence of our Muslim neighbors.

Consider the example of Turia. She lived almost as a prisoner in her in-laws' apartment. It took us months to meet her. When a visitor appeared, she would not join the group, even for a meal. My wife compares women in these situations to Cinderella. How unfortunate that they don't just exist in fairy tales! Some aspects of the lives of Muslim young women in the West are illustrated by the case described in *Not Without My Daughter* by Betty Mahmoody.[13] Recognize that the situation examined there is specifically that of an American married to an Iranian Muslim.

The principle behind this behavior touches on the *haraam* system of Islam.[14] Much of Islamic practice among North Africans in France focuses on what is forbidden (*haraam*) and what is allowed (*halaal*).

A glimpse at traditional housing in many Muslim countries may help you better understand the mindset. Traditional houses are built with few windows on the street side. Those that exist are small and barred. In the interior of the building is a large courtyard which forms the center of the dwelling. This is completely enclosed. In this fashion, the women are protected from the view of others. Special rooms are set up for hospitality. Guests are never shown the entire apartment or house. Yet they are made to feel most welcome. Before we dismiss this as part of a distant past, remember that families on vacation regularly return to their homelands. When they do, most plunge right back into these *Arab quarters* where the majority of the population live. Your Muslim friend's lodgings may still reflect some aspect of this culture.

Male-Female Relationships

Relationships between men and women remain some of the most difficult for Westerners to understand. They represent, nonetheless, a key in reaching the women of Islam in Western countries. Understanding gender relations also helps in relating to Muslim families. A social *faux pas* can create a lasting barrier. For an excellent discussion of these cultural aspects, see *Childhood in the Moslem World*[15] by pioneer missionary and scholar Samuel Zwemer. Written at the beginning of the century, this book is still full of insights into the importance of reaching the mother. She holds in her mind and heart the destiny of the next generation.

Religious Rites and Behaviors

As non-Muslims, we seek to win our way into the hearts of our Muslim neighbors. We need to examine some of the ways to enter into the world in which our friends live. Of course, actual membership in any group of second generation Muslims in a Western country is determined by birth. There are, therefore, no *rites of passage*. Certain rites appear, however, in maintaining one's position as a proper member of their society. Try to understand how they integrate into their own group. You will see more clearly what steps you may take to become close to that same group.

Some rites that are key to becoming part of a Muslim grouping in the West include:

- Fasting during the month of Ramadan after reaching puberty.

- Abstaining from eating pork. This is no small feat in Western secondary schools. As Muslims have more say in local communities, they lobby to gain concessions for their dietary restrictions.

- Circumcision for boys.

- For many, participation in various magical practices (e.g., seeing a sorcerer with one's mother if there is a prevailing sickness).

- Observing the various social codes (e.g., hospitality in serving tea or coffee to guests).

- The Pilgrimage to Mecca.

The believer in Christ examines the place of rites, rituals, and religious practices among his people. The pilgrimage to Mecca looms on the Islamic horizon as the unique means of establishing one's place in Islam and local society. Those who make the pilgrimage are given special notoriety, a title of honor (*Hajji*), and wear special dress on numerous festive occasions. If they are too verbose about their experiences, however, their fellow Muslims may despise them. There is an Arab proverb that says: "May God save us from three [things]: disaster, tribulation and the pilgrims."

You should note that the first and last items in the preceding list are two of the five *Pillars* of Islam. These are required rituals for a practicing Muslim. A biblical understanding of fasting and hospitality, for example, can help us find acceptance by our friend's family.

Remember the struggle over the care of widows in Acts 6? Peter, John and the other disciples took a bold stand for Christ. The widows were being cut off from their own community as a reaction of persecution. What will it mean if your friend follows Christ? Because of the Muslim's background, forces of persecution often arise. Pray that your brother and sister will be able to continue to live for Jesus right in their own circle of family and friends.[16]

On one occasion, my wife and I visited California. A repeated message droned on in the Los Angeles International Airport: "Do not leave your bags unattended." Be careful not to leave your Muslim friend unattended. His or her interest in Christ will certainly be challenged. He will then need your friendship and prayers more than ever.

Said's brother-in-law is a prime example of an outsider coming into the family unit. He is a Tunisian Arab married to Said's Kabyle sister. Yet he is the congenial host at major family gatherings because he has a large home in the modest suburbs of their large city. Although he is retired from French government service, this produces no stigma as far as I could observe. Said's uncle fought during World War II in the Algerian (then French) colonial army. He spoke of this experience with great pride. Military service acts as a bonding point between North Africans like these and the French among whom they live. The requirement to serve in two armies (the country of their parent's origin and that of their own nationality), however, can prove a real uprooting experience for them. Matters such as these may provide points of contact where you can become linked in mutual interest with Muslims around you.

Group Activities in Western Muslim Society

Muslim youth are usually integrated more or less into Western society. Consequently, we find less group-wide activity among them here than would be so in their family's country of origin. This probably varies among Western countries and also according to the race and nation of the people. I have observed that some Berbers appear more French in their outlook than my Arab friends from similar backgrounds.

Gatherings tend to focus around special family occasions (e.g., marriage, birth, death). Muslim feast days also provide a social focus. Some of these may be:

- Evening feasting and visiting during Ramadan.

- The Sheep Feast (*al-'iid al-kabiir*), where the parents will buy a sheep.

- Departure or return from the Hajj to Mecca.

As with other Islamic traditions, careful observance is declining, particularly among working men. It is not easy to fast when one does not live in an Islamic society. Work drones on, with no thought on the part of the boss to encourage the Muslim's religious duties. The difficulty grows when the lunar calendar of Islam puts the Ramadan fast month in the hot summer months.

You need to ask God's Holy Spirit for discernment to see what lies beneath the religious practices of your Muslim friends and their families. At first, some individuals may appear to be motivated by a zealous commitment to Islam. They may, however, turn out to be driven by popular rather than pure Islam. The motive for the Sheep Feast is, in many cases, self-gratification, self-merit and, to some degree, self-significance. Some give parts of the sheep to the poor. They also may give to friends who are not Muslim in order to gain merit or a good reputation.

The underlying motive for Ramadan observance may be a desire for status (also true to a lesser degree in the Sheep Feast). This may also be true of the non-consumption of pork or alcohol. The alcohol ban is less practiced by male youths. Many of these issues are dealt with in the helpful writings of Christian authors like Phil Parshall and Bill Musk.

The family unit is the key part of the attachment of our Muslim friend to the cultural milieu. How can *you* enter into your friend's world?

Success in Penetrating the Muslim's World

What is the key in finding true, lasting acceptance and fulfillment? We long for it; so do they. Acceptance comes with entry into the Body of Christ. Christian fellowship will fill that great need of loneliness and that thirst for acceptance. Paul ends many of his letters with a list of Christian friends for whom he prays (e.g., Colossians 4 and Romans 16). Friendship is the key to penetration. Friendship is also a time-consuming task, but not an impossible one. Ask God to give you one person with whom you may invest your love and concern. One of our greatest faults is to drop people. Thankfully, our Lord does not do that with us. He has called us to be like Him.

Can believers in the Lord Jesus Christ succeed in penetrating their Muslim friends' circle of family and friends? Certainly; was Jesus not the Son of Man? Jesus was an *outsider* from Heaven, yet He perfectly identified with us and our cultures. How do we fulfill our commission to go and make disciples (Mark 16:15; Matthew 28:18–19)? We need to acquire skill in understanding our Muslim friend's culture. We might discover that the culture itself can actually *help* us. We should become listeners and learners as we are with our friend. We must avoid the pitfall of rushing in too rapidly with our own Western mindset. God first directed His message to people in an Eastern cultural mold. An attitude of respect is like a ticket to enter that world.

You will probably observe, as I have, that outsiders are treated with great respect if they are brought into the family circle. Accepted opinion often tells us that Muslim people are biased and difficult to get to know. Often the very opposite is true. Why? The remarkable Arab customs of hospitality come into play. Especially in their own countries, Arabs may go into debt to receive a Western guest in style. We should be careful, within our means, to reciprocate. Of course, we can never become full members of the group of our Muslim friend. Ultimately, it is a racial one, entered by birth. In spite of this, we may become very close to them as we allow the love of the Spirit of God to flow through us.

Lawrence of Arabia once remarked that, given a strong leader, the Arabs are invincible. He illustrated this saying himself. Those who followed Lawrence accepted him, even though he was a foreigner. His intense interest in their language and lifestyle won the Arabs' allegiance. One Arab Christian scholar likes to cite this example to help outsiders witness to Arabs. God can use you to do the same, and even go much further. As you win your friends, they become sisters or brothers in the Lord Jesus Christ.

We must remember that in Islam, religion is both spiritual and socio-political. This is illustrated by the Muslim saying: *al-islaam, huuwa diin wa dunyaa* (Islam is both religion and worldly existence). We are seeking to develop skill in the use of spiritual tools which God provides for us. As we do, we can help the Muslim find forgiveness of sin in Christ and integrate into a local evangelical church.

We have examined building materials used in constructing the Church. We must witness according to the characteristics and *cultural* context of our Muslim friends. The next step will require careful examination of their *religious* world. We will also need help in discerning the occult world that holds so many Muslims — young and old — in its vise-like grip.

For Reflection

How well do I understand the family of my Muslim friend? What cases mentioned above apply? Which ones do not?

For Action

1. Make a prayer list of all the members of your friend's family. Ask the Holy Spirit to direct you to key people for whom you may concentrate prayer.

2. Seek to visit not only with your friend, but also with the family. Concentrate on winning the confidence of the parents, through a godly, Spirit-filled life.

3. Talk to your friend about the meaning of Islam. Write down the practices that seem most important. What does Scripture say about these areas?

For Additional Study

1. Consider the relationships of those who came to Christ in the last part of John 1. How does this apply to your Muslim friend?

2. Reflect on the *firstborn son* teaching in the Old Testament (e.g., the choice of Joseph over his brothers, Jacob over Esau). What do these exceptions tell you about working within a Muslim family?

6

Winning in
Spiritual Warfare

**Many seek magical means
to attain everyday ends.
...There is need for a manifestation of
the Lord Jesus Christ's power in the lives of all.**

Remember Jesus' encounter with the Samaritan woman? Jesus addressed the woman at the well (a rather notorious Samaritan sinner) at her point of need: water (John 4). Satisfaction was her deepest longing. He spoke to Nicodemus' felt need in a very different way (John 3). Our Lord opened up a deep theological concept for this prominent Jewish thinker. Nicodemus' heart-longing was for closeness to God. The first part of any message we communicate is like the point of an arrow. If the point is sharp and clean, it will penetrate to the very heart-need of our friend. Each Muslim is possessed by strong currents of felt need. Our approach should speak to that felt need.

A witness to a Muslim neighbor needs the discernment that only the Holy Spirit of God can give. How do we know how to approach and reach the person God has placed before us? We must understand our friend's social and cultural world. The heart of the matter, however, is to reach his or her heart. This inevitably leads to spiritual opposition from Satan, the soul's enemy. We need to gain victory in spiritual warfare.

What does your friend actually believe and feel? Obviously individuals differ, but the illustrative outline (Table 2, below) is generally accurate. Note that the *first generation* lives in a world that uses magic. Many seek magical means to attain everyday ends (health, happy marriage, a job, status). These may well dominate the spiritual realms of their lives. In the *second generation* this does not appear to be true. Their parents, however, are still involved in the everyday lives of their children. This involvement is much greater than it would be for the average Westerner. Many young people have, at the urging of parents, involuntarily participated in the world of sorcery during their childhood. Some of these satanic practices may have marked them for life.

Group	Prime Motivation	Appropriate Message
Young Muslim Women	Finding a happy marriage, independence	Christ loves and frees her
Young Muslim Men	Achieving status, overcoming rejection	He can have position in Christ and a place with the people of God
Parents of the First Generation	Key goals obtained through power (often occult)	Christ has power over all evil that may hinder these goals

Table 2: Felt Needs and God's Answer

There is need for a manifestation of the Lord Jesus Christ's power in the lives of all. He conquered the world of Satan and demons, and the evil that goes with it. This world is starkly real, in spite of younger people's outward denial. The words of Jesus speak clearly: "So if the Son sets you free, you will be free indeed" (John 8:36).

In a previous chapter we briefly sampled some Muslim practices in France. We especially studied their social impact. These practices probably represent typical beliefs of Muslims in other Western countries as well. The significance of these beliefs is like the trackless ways of the Sahara Desert. The concerned but uninformed Christian witness may lose his or her way. Our goal here is to gain victory in the spiritual world in which our Muslim neighbor lives.

What inner and outer qualities do our friends manifest? Muslims in Western countries, as do people everywhere, often possess *a form of godliness* while *denying its power*. Paul describes this in 2 Timothy 3:2–5. What are the various spiritual implications for the life of a young Muslim? The answer will help us understand the faith of the *second generation*. We will also discern the underlying patchwork of motives and felt needs. In the case of many, belief mingles strongly with unbelief. A militant, materialistic, or political exterior may camouflage a very firm commitment to seek help from a healer or medium. What do our Muslim friends really believe?[17]

Belief Grows Out of the Soil

Belief grows out of the soil of personal, inner conviction about the hidden, spiritual world. Muslims live day after day in this world, even in the sophisticated West. To many outside observers, this belief appears paradoxical. On one hand, they adopt the patterns of the European or American society around them. They are also often greatly concerned with the accumulation of material wealth. This makes them appear to have no spiritual interest.

On the other hand, most believe profoundly in the invisible spiritual world. What do I mean by these statements?

A young Algerian wrote to us of how Allah helped her to pass the driver's license examination. This perceived intervention loomed large in her thinking. Biblical conceptions of the same truths, gained by personal study, would have the same impact. This world view brings God into every area of life, microscopic and macroscopic. Our familiar *secular* and *sacred* distinctions do not even exist in their thinking. How does this invisible world, often with occult overtones, mesh with daily life?

It is true that Muslim youths in Western countries unconsciously absorb much of the prevailing secular view of life. This is true whatever their educational ability and level. To paraphrase Francis Schaeffer, they feel that even if God is *there*, He is certainly *silent* on the daily issues of their lives. They need an occult fast fix, by medium, astrologer, or magic charm.[18] As the Apostle Paul found that the sophisticated Greek city of Athens was "full of idols" (Acts 17:16), so the *second generation* has various spiritual schemes to help them obtain what they want in life. Add to this mix the influence of parental beliefs, and those of aunts, uncles, other direct family members, and occasional acquaintances among militant Muslim young people.

Understanding Different Kinds of Belief: A Sampler

Let's look at examples of what some Muslims believe. You may discover some similarity with what your friend believes. One North African Christian friend states:

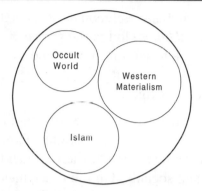

Figure 10: A Variety of Beliefs

My family is not fanatical about Islam, praise the Lord. My mother practices her religion, but she listens to the gospel. The same is basically true of my brother-in-law (an older man of the first generation). However, he does periodically attack what the Bible says." Then he compares his case to others. "Young people that hang around in gangs are neither Muslim nor Christian. But when you speak to them of Jesus (*yasuu' al-masiiH*, he then wrote in Arabic), they wave the flag of Islam. They have a cultural Islam that they don't understand very well."

How do young Muslims draw on their parents' beliefs? They flaunt their Islamic faith. Yet, in reality, it is heavily colored by an occult world view. They seek to manipulate the supernatural in many details of life. They long to *control, rather than to be controlled* by God. Does a husband fall ill? He did not follow the rituals as he should have. Does a man's wife stop loving him? Probably her family put a curse on their marriage. Is a woman unable to have a baby? Popular Islam says that she needs to visit the *marabout* (sorcerer) to obtain help from the spirit world.

"Where does Islam's theory of submission to the will of Allah come in?" We can legitimately ask them this question. Rather than "buttering God up" by our manipulation, we need to "seek first his kingdom and his righteousness" (Matthew 6:33). The Arabic cry *allaahu akbar*, "God is the Greatest," is a fact. In saying this, we can come to Him in prayer and discover His will for us. Yet so many Muslim youths, when they think of God, see Him merely as a kind of figurehead.

We see in Figure 10 how small circles of seemingly contradictory beliefs can exist within the larger circle of the Muslims' lives. They adopt a dual philosophy. On the one hand, they want to be happy materially and socially. On the other hand, they long to be distinctly *Arab*. That includes whatever family customs are convenient, along with some formal Islamic practices.

To illustrate these varied beliefs, I would like to paraphrase an article from *Urban Mission*.[19] The quotations, while not verbatim, represent actual conversations with Muslim North Africans.

Question	Answer
What do you think about the place of God in our lives today?	**A Factory Worker:** Well, you know, sir, I am a believer all right, but I just don't practice my faith anymore. It's not easy to fast here in a foreign country, especially when Ramadan comes in the hot summer months. Your boss still expects you to work as you always have.
What does Islam mean to you?	**A College Student:** I was very proud when I was able to start fasting like the rest of my family … Of course, I don't know Arabic, so I don't read the Qur'an. There are many things I don't know about my religion. But I am a Muslim. Am I not a [he names his country of origin]?
What do you think of your husband's acceptance of Jesus Christ as his Savior and Lord?	**A Young Wife and Mother:** That is just fine for him. There are many things I respect about his faith. But I could never take that step. In my culture, the women are expected to carry on the Muslim traditions, even sometimes when their husbands don't believe in Allah. Think of how I would be ostracized! Then, too, I'm afraid. My grandfather is involved in occult practices and has real power. What would happen to me if I left the fold of Islam?

What did you think of your reading of the Bible over the last months?	**A Former Teacher and a Learned Muslim:** I especially like the first part [the Old Testament]. But I have trouble understanding how you Christians can say that someone else could pay for our sins. I read the Qur'an and pray. After all, both of our religions are the same in the essentials.
Did you have a chance to hear the Bible cassettes I left with you?	**An Algerian Wife in the Hospital:** Oh, I just loved them! I have heard them all. These are such good words. Can you come to see me more often?

Table 3: Variations in Belief

The figure (below) describes beliefs of the variegated North African population in France. Many Muslims in other Western countries follow this model. To the left are the politically active. Their faith, if they have any, is a form of deism. To the right are the religiously motivated, such as the Muslim Brotherhood (*al-ikhwaan al-muslimiin*). Both of these extremes are active on university campuses. The ideas of the militant group exert increasing influence on the immigrants who live in France.

A Warning

Any purely external look at the various religious beliefs of our Muslim friend may too easily lead us astray. We are tempted to accept surface impressions. When visiting with a young Algerian on a street corner, for example, we may hear echoes of an *orthodox*, or *Qur'anic Islam*. This is to the right in the spectrum of belief. A Muslim may exalt any one of a number of common practices of *orthodox Islam* portrayed in the media.

POLITICAL ISLAM   MYSTICAL ISLAM   QUR'ANIC ISLAM

Figure 11: A Spectrum of Belief

It will help us to review for a moment some of the facets of *orthodox Islam*. We might call this Islam's public face. In summary, practices more prevalent among Muslims living in the West are:

- Observance of Ramadan.
- Mosque attendance.
- Observance of one or more Qur'anic dietary laws (e.g., abstention from pork or alcohol).
- An intention to accomplish the Pilgrimage.

Other practices are:

- Learning the Arabic language, primarily to facilitate reading of the Qur'an.
- Observance of the seemingly strict moral code regarding women and marriage, especially when it is compared with the loose moral atmosphere in Western society.
- Observance of any one of a variety of family customs that are both social and religious.

Let me illustrate. A Western Christian desires to communicate faith in Christ to a Muslim neighbor. The Christian notices that the friend piously observes Ramadan each year. Nothing is eaten or drunk from sunrise to sunset. On sounding the depths of the motives of this Muslim friend, however, the Christian might find the unexpected. The Muslim may keep Ramadan in order to barter God's help in dealing with evil or sickness. For an excellent discussion of this, see Bill Musk's article on Popular Islam.[20]

Be careful not to believe the media image of *high* or *orthodox Islam* while ignoring the underlying base of *popular Islam*. What are your friend's beliefs, and what are the presuppositions that underlie them? We will now seek to explore this terrain more fully.

People Who Live in Glass Houses

"People who live in glass houses should not throw stones." Underlying much of the popular belief among Muslims is traditional religion, more technically termed *animism*. Animism believes that the *force* (so-called "life force") is everywhere. A person need only call upon the force to use it. This represents the Devil's counterfeit of the Christian's great source of strength: "But you will receive power when the Holy Spirit comes on you" (Acts 1:8). The source of this resurrection power is a person, the Holy Spirit. The book of Acts reveals this throughout, and for that reason is a good text to use in witnessing to followers of Islam.

The animist world view pervades the Muslim world where the saving power of Christ (Romans 1:13–18) is relatively unknown. Even then, God's power to save cannot be restrained.

Reflecting on our own history, however, will remind us that we have no reason to approach the Muslim with pride. Our Western culture has fared no better before the powers of darkness. Popular belief that draws from the world of spirits is an integral part of our own past and present experience. Take the historical example of the peoples of France. The Celtic era, and successive eras of French history offers many examples of the evocation of spirit forces. The same is true throughout the histories of England, Germany and all of the other countries of so-called "enlightened" Europe. Psychic experience is flourishing today throughout Europe and North America, which some feel is experiencing a revival in reverse.[21]

The *second generation* of North African immigrants is influenced by this Western occult world as well as their own. In September 1986, Arab World Ministries placed its first team in Lyon, the second largest city in France. The aim was to work among the sizable Muslim population there. Once, my son John and I were visiting in a monastery near Grenoble, in the French Alps. A Catholic priest living there told us how people in remote mountain areas surrounding Lyon still practice pagan beliefs. They seemed untouched by Christianity. Lyon also has the reputation of being the center of occultism in France. How significant when we remember that it was an early center of Christianity with its share of martyrs. In many places in the Western world, the old occult ways are resurfacing. Young Muslims may blend practices from Islam with such teachings as they detect all around them.

The *parents* of second-generation Muslims in Europe were uprooted from North Africa and other lands and transplanted to their host countries. They have also been uprooted from the power and influence of localized spirit forces in their native lands. In time of need, they may go back to their homelands to obtain a magic writing or potion. When we see how corrupt these occult roots are, we can be grateful that God has used this whole process of dramatic change. He is giving these Muslim peoples a new sense of need. Separation like this also makes some of the *second generation* much more open to the gospel of the "God who changes not" (Malachi 3:6). He is the God of power, who created the worlds and opened the Red Sea. We must bear in mind, however, that Muslims are not indifferent to the presence of spirit forces in their adopted lands. Nor have they stopped seeking occult, demonic help in their adopted Western countries.

Principles for Victory Over Occult Islam
Occultic popular Islam is built on deception.
The new family of God provides a powerful supportive web of relationships.
Through Christ, the new believer has victory over Satan.
Exercising our victory in Christ requires taking a stand against the forces of occultism.

Table 4: Christ's Victory Over Occultism

Our failure to recognize and deal with the occult is the one most evident weakness in the witness of Western Christians to Muslims. I would like to draw up some principles for experiencing Christ's victory over this occult reality. These will help you to win the battle over the occult powers of Islam.

Occult Islam Is Built on Deception

The Bible speaks of the Devil as the "father of lies." Satan lies about his own nature, seeking to appear as an angel of light (Isaiah 14:3–17; Ezekiel 28:1–19). What was the first reaction of Adam and Eve when they disobeyed God? This is important to us, since they were the first sinners on earth: our first parents attempted to cover their sin. The word *occult* means *hidden* or *concealed*. Spiritual cover-up!

Islam seeks to hide its true inner nature. We may try to deal with our Muslim neighbor only on the formal level of orthodox Islam. Our friend may like to be admired for Muslim belief. Yet this is often merely a dressed-up religious façade. If we are taken in by this, we will never be able to minister to the real need of our friend. We must rather reach within, by the Spirit from above, sent by God. How different He is from a spirit from beneath. Is it not significant that He is also called the *Holy* Spirit? What a contrast to the twisted path that young people follow, often unknowingly. Satan's aim is to make them unholy.

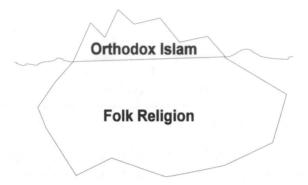

Figure 12: The Iceberg

My favorite illustration about this world is that of the iceberg. The outer, visible part of it is like orthodox, outward Islam. It may appear very beautiful to behold. Yet what we see is not the full reality. The vast majority of the bulk of the iceberg is hidden under the surface. Popular Islam is the moving force behind the belief and practice of so many Muslims we meet. This is true of young and old, educated and uneducated.

We must not be deceived into ignoring the reality of satanic power in the life of our friends. They must see the truth of God's Word in its teaching about this occult world. Begin with the story of the temptation of Adam and Eve. Then speak of Christ's temptation. The message of both Old and New Testaments will combine to confront your friend with the truth about the Devil. And it will especially help to reveal the reality of victory through Christ's death and resurrection.

The Family of God Provides New Relationships

The world which surrounds Muslims makes our task of ministering to them more difficult. The social structure that hedges them in protects this hidden, occult part of their belief. The enormous benefits provided by the security of the extended Christian family become evident: the prayers of God's people protect the believer from the assaults of the enemy. Converts seeking freedom from the occult network all around them need prayer all the more.

The Apostle John speaks of the relationship of believers in Christ in family terms. He addresses the recipients of his first letter as *dear children* (1 John 2:1, 18) and God as "the Father" of that family (3:1, 5:1). Relations within an extended family unit or other grouping are called web relations. In our spiritual family, this web becomes a tie to hold us in focus on Christ. We need this all the more as spiritual warfare develops around the new believer's relationship to the Lord Jesus. In the Muslims' milieu, the family web may become a channel for the gospel, passing from one relative (one strand of the web) to another. Opposition, however, may also follow the web. Soon many members of the family may set themselves against the believer. The picture further clouds with occult methods (such as spells, fetishes, and harmful potions). Social pressure also makes resistance seem impossible.

We need to look at the way God can use the web. The web of family and society that surrounds our Muslim friends can influence our witness to them of God's truth.

Kinza is a Moroccan sister-in-Christ. She faced losing the security of her family's acceptance. In following Christ, she realized there would be a break with occult practices. These formed an integral part of her family life. The close family fabric of her world would work against her. Family members would try to eliminate her influence, much as we would want to remove a foreign object lodged in our eye.

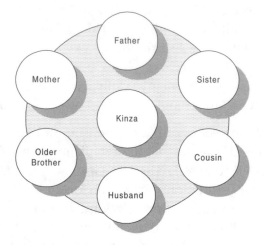

Figure 13: Web of Relationships

Kinza envisaged all this as she weighed her decision for Christ. As she followed Him, several believers befriended her. They became like a new family to her. Among these new friends was an older couple who knew her country well. They also had personal experience in dealing with the reality of satanic power. One day, a burning of occult books took place on Kinza's balcony. It reminded us of Acts 19. Then God's power prevailed. The church is God's *umma* or community of people. Kinza's church became a place of worship and security. The spiritual influence of God's people held evil powers in check.

Western Christians often fail to realize how fragile and exposed new converts from Islam are. Their community protection and security may be seeping away like precious water in the dry soil of an arid land. Will the local church rise up and close ranks of love and compassion around the new believer? Is it prepared to minister to the whole person, thus forming a new family? Our experience has demonstrated that such solidarity may surprise the new believer's family and friends. They suddenly become aware of a new power — *agape*.

The message passes along this web of relationships that the followers of Jesus Christ become a true *umma*. They are a dynamic, powerful community. A new protection sets itself in place, like a life-giving atmosphere over the new convert. The believer no longer needs to resort to the charms or occult pronouncements of the family. We will learn more about this vital need when we consider the local church.

In Christ, the New Believer Has Victory Over Satan

Believers in Christ from a Muslim background may feel spiritually crippled. This comes from the intense effort of the enemy to hinder Christ's vital work among Muslims. Colossians 2:13–15 (and its context) is a powerful word from God to all of us here. Our version says: "having disarmed the powers and authorities." The French and Arabic versions use the word "skinned." I like to point out that a skinned animal is not in much of a position to fight back. I remind my friends of the sheepskin rugs that we enjoy walking on in North Africa. The Apostle Paul often emphasizes this message of victory over demonic forces. You find this repeated in Colossians and its companion letter, Ephesians. Study these to lay hold on Jesus' victory for yourself and to teach it to your friend.

These letters were written to two local churches in two cities of Asia Minor. This reminds us again of the new relationships provided by God in the church. Your own local church should be the spiritual springboard from which you will reach out to your friend. The church will help you in raising the shield of faith as attacks come from the enemy. As Muslim converts become a part of the church community, they will know real victory over occult forces. They will be able to say with Paul: "But thanks be to God, who always leads us in triumphal procession in Christ and through us spreads everywhere the fragrance of the knowledge of him" (2 Corinthians 2:14). Young believers will eventually touch their own network of social, family relationships. God's Spirit will draw others, as they see the prevailing power of this new Christian over the dark occult world. They will long for the power of God that we possess in the person of Christ.

Victory Requires Taking a Stand Against Occultism

Some examples given in this chapter and elsewhere in the manual will help you to grasp how the gospel message penetrates this hidden world. It touches every *second generation* Muslim that I have ever known. We must allow God's Holy Spirit to lead us into this spiritual warfare. Then God will bring our Muslim friend to the knowledge of God's triumphant Son. We must never forget to take our stand against the powers of darkness. We will discover that we do so with the *true power* that flows from the risen Christ (Acts 1:8; Philippians 3:10).

We need to pray for one another that we may "know Christ and the power of his resurrection." In 1 Corinthians 15:58, Paul exhorts us to "stand firm. Let nothing move you." It is no coincidence that this also follows the Bible's fullest exposition of the resurrection of Jesus Christ. On that basis, we can encourage our Muslim friends to receive Christ as their Victor. Then they can experience this victory as well. Using this tool of victory in warfare, God helps us to discern the spiritual needs of our friends, much like a builder who chooses carefully the materials to develop later.

For Reflection

1. How well do I know the background of my friend? Have I interacted only on the superficial level of orthodox Islam? Am I becoming close enough to discover the occult substratum of popular Islam which binds and controls?

2. What are the specific practices that keep Muslim young people in bondage? Do they in fact consult with a marabout, medium, sorcerer? Do they use magic formulas to obtain what they want in time of need? Remember that it will take time to build a trust relationship with your friend where some of these hidden issues will come to light.

3. How well do I know our Book, inspired by the Holy Spirit? He gives true victory over evil, unclean, lying spirits. You are a part of the *People of the Book*. Reflect on cases of Jesus casting out demons in the Gospels. Reflect on the use of magic books or formulas by those among whom Paul ministered (Acts 19:13–20). Whatever tools may help you in this manual, the *indispensable* tool is the Word of God, wielded by the Spirit of God. God enables us, through Scripture, to discern the evil powers arrayed against us. Then the Spirit unleashes the greater power of God against them.

4. Do I really *know experientially* the *power* of the Holy Spirit in my daily life? Acts, the book of church history in the Bible, is also a book on missions. Furthermore, the book on missions also demonstrates the Spirit's power in life situations. The path to this power lies through obedience to the commands of the Lord. Acts illustrates *power encounters* in the missionary ministry of Christ's apostles. Victory over the demon possessing a slave girl (Acts 16:16–18) is just one example.

5. How important is the supernatural world to your Muslim friend? Could the miracles of Jesus, showing His power and per-

son, be a means of approach? In this whole area of the spirit world, remember to keep your eyes focused on the Lord Jesus Christ, not on any occult practice or personal struggle your friend may be experiencing. Take one look at the situation, and nine at Christ (Hebrews 12:1–2; 1 Corinthians 15).

6. What specific practices seem to exert a strong, if not controlling influence over the life of your Muslim friend? Do you see any evidence of the occult world coming through as you speak with the person? Next to each one you list, add biblical principles that could help your friend to see God's truth.

I have reflected a great deal on the suggestion that perhaps the key method of approaching Muslims would be our common ground of fear. They are afraid of unknown spirit powers, of spells and charms being used against them. The Old Testament speaks often of the hidden world they fear. We should speak openly about this fear. This will build a bridge between us. We should share how Christ has conquered the fears that once gripped us. Elijah encountered the prophets of Baal with the power of God (1 Kings 18:16–40). Those false prophets consistently used occult means to manipulate situations. The Lord can overpower Satan in our lives just as He did in those days.

For Action

A Christian decides to reach out to a Muslim neighbor, seeking the help of Christian friends. As they persevere together in prayer, they could use this ministry strategy:

1. Prepare for *confrontation* with evil powers. Christ in you is your hope of victory. You may fast and pray to know God's time to confront these powers in the individuals whom God puts in your path. Mark Bubeck gives us some excellent guidelines in *The Adversary*. Also read *The Bondage Breaker* by Neil T. An-

derson. We should be ready to engage in spiritual combat. Deliverance may come suddenly or through a long ministry of prayer and teaching. One North African woman found deliverance in Christ from satanic oppression only after a long period of prayer and study in the Bible.

2. Seek for *balanced Bible teaching* on the spirit world in your local church community. Formal teaching about power confrontation in the two Testaments should have a place. We also should discuss the hidden occult world informally. In this way, we create an atmosphere of sensitivity to the path of victory outlined in the Word.

3. *Listen* to believers from Muslim background. Virtually all of them have grown up in this occult context. Some still live there, by virtue of their Muslim families. Their input makes our prayer and Bible study come alive. Encourage them to speak and write materials adapted to their own people.

4. Keep your team of *prayer partners informed*. Who could covenant to join you in prayer as you witness for Christ to a Muslim? North Africa began to open up spiritually in the 1960s. Some eighty years of intense and growing prayer preceded this work of God. Many are convinced that this preparation explains what God has done today. A leader of one Christian group working among Muslims in France stated: "Our first and only effective strategy is *prayer*." The same is true of the city where you live. Remember how Paul ends his chapter on spiritual armor with five references to *prayer* (Ephesians 6:18–20).

5. *Read and share* some of the existing books that deal with victory over the occult in Islam. I have been helped by Jessie Penn-Lewis' *War on the Saints*. See also the writings of Mark Bubeck, Phil Parshall and others cited in the Bibliography. Sam Schlorff's *Discipleship in Islamic Society* includes a section on spiritual conflict.

For Additional Study

Study passages in the Gospels where Jesus dealt with demonic forces. Draw practical lessons from Matthew 12:24–32, Mark 5:1–20 (and parallels in Matthew 8:28–34 and Luke 8:26–39) and Mark 9:38–41. What lessons do you learn for today? How will these apply as you help your Muslim friend to find the "freedom for which Christ has set us free" (Galatians 5:1)? Compare also John 8:32 ("the truth will set you free") with John 8:36 ("If the Son sets you free, you will be free indeed"). What importance does this truth have in your witness? How may it help to deliver our friends from attacks of the enemy?

7

Discipleship

**Follow-up is a personal process of
teaching and training designed to equip
the new convert to become an active member
of a Christian community.**

Have you noticed a progression as you have worked through this manual? Initially, we considered our Muslim neighbor as one who is outside the Body of Christ. Next, we looked at principles that can apply both to unbelievers and new believers. We learned how to approach our friend with the message of Christ. And we stressed that when the light of Christ dawns in the Muslim's heart, that person becomes our brother or sister. We might now ask, "What is next?"

Matthew, the Evangelist, gives his own gospel presentation. This Gospel helps many Muslims because it reflects an oriental manner of thinking. At the end, Matthew sums up his message by quoting Jesus: "All authority in heaven and on earth has been given to me. Therefore *go and make disciples* of all nations, baptizing them ... and teaching them" (Matthew 28:18–20). In this chapter we will try to answer the question: "How can new believers learn more about Christ and find their places in the local church?"

Many new converts from Islam have fallen by the wayside because of a lack of teaching. In the euphoria of the decision, we may fail to build a foundation. This tool — discipling — is like a carpenter's plane. Teaching a new believer is like smoothing out the rough places on a piece of wooden furniture. We instruct this new Christian in basic principles of godly living. Then our friend finds help in the new community, a local church.

Most of us learn how to do follow-up as we develop a friendship with a new believer from our own culture. It involves a listening ear, a tender heart, a biblically trained mind, and many cups of coffee! You might think: "But *teaching* is the job of the *pastor*." You are partly correct if you add to your statement "and the local church." Consider two facts. First, you are a friend to the new convert. You gained this person's trust. Secondly, many new Christians find integration into a church difficult. How much more if most members of the church are from a different cultural background. We claim the presence of Christ with us always (Matthew 28:20), a promise that is certainly ours. But the teaching and discipling responsibility referred to (Matthew 28:18–19) is also ours.

A Definition of Discipleship

I would recommend the following definition of discipleship or follow-up:

> Follow-up is a personal process of teaching and training designed to equip the new convert to become an active member of a Christian community. From this community, the convert reaches out as a witness to those around. In this

way, the new believer becomes one who is "qualified to teach others" (2 Timothy 2:2).[22]

Pause for a moment to consider each part of this definition. ***Personal*** indicates that you, as spiritual parent or friend, must give of yourself to the new Christian. Read through the Gospels again and see how much time Jesus spent with the Twelve. In the beginning, Jesus related to a group of friends gathered around Him. He healed Simon's mother-in-law (Luke 4:38–39). He called a special, intimate group of twelve disciples from a larger group of those who followed Him (Matthew 4:18–22). He drew Levi by the magnetism of God's love (Luke 5:27–28); this self-seeking tax collector discovered "what a friend he had in Jesus."

Follow-up is first ***teaching***. Matthew tells us of the great teaching discourses of Jesus (see Matthew 5–7, and 21:28–25:46). Jesus' disciples listened in the foreground as the Lord taught the crowds. They caught His every word, as well as the reaction of His listeners. This was no mere sanitized seminar on principles of teaching. This aspect of Jesus' work stood out clearly in the thinking of Nicodemus, himself a teacher of the Jews (John 3:10).

Training differs from teaching. In Paul's last letter to his own disciple, Timothy, he sheds light on this distinction. In 2 Timothy 3:16, Paul separates teaching from training by two other concepts: *rebuking* and *correcting*. Life change (which the two words evoke) lies on the path of teaching. Only then does teaching become *training in righteousness*.

Try to begin your instruction of the new believer with an overview of the Old Testament. Draw comparisons with the New Testament as you work through it. One example you might give is the contrast between Psalms and its neighbor in the canon, Proverbs. Psalms overflows with doctrinal teaching on such subjects as the person and worship of God and the sinfulness of the human race. Proverbs puts essential elements of this teaching into pithy little sayings. These stick to the palate of people from Eastern background just like the honey used in Arab pastries. Psalms is basically a teaching book,

Key Elements of Discipleship
Personal Relationship
Teaching the Truth of God
Training in Righteousness
Community Life
Witness to Others

Table 5: Key Elements of Discipleship

applied to worship and prayer. Proverbs fleshes that out in countless situations of everyday life.

Community is one destination of your help for this new believer. Jesus' disciples formed the initial community to which Jesus referred in Matthew 16:18. "On this rock I will build my church," Jesus told them, referring both to Himself as the foundation of the community and also more obliquely to Peter, its first leader. The small band of disciples moved out with God's Holy Spirit to become the church that developed in Acts of the Apostles.

Witness is the second destination of follow-up. The Apostle John often uses this word in his writings. Follow John's story and you find how the Twelve moved from being learners to becoming witnesses. They held in their hearts and hands an authoritative message of forgiveness (John 20:23): "If you forgive anyone his sins, they are forgiven; if you do not forgive them, they are not forgiven."

Jesus' last word to His disciples echoes like a trumpet call: *Follow Me!* (John 21:19, 22). They followed *Him*, because He first followed *them* in personal teaching and training.

The Process of Follow-up

Teaching God's Truth

We witness to our Muslim neighbors because Jesus sent us. Notice again Matthew's version of the Great Commission; Jesus says, "All authority in heaven and on earth has been given to me. Therefore go and *make disciples of all nations*" (Matthew 28:18–20). How do new disciples grow into obedience of "everything I have commanded you" (28:20b)? The answer is, as they follow Christ in baptism, as Jesus commands in verse 19. *Teaching* also plays a vital role. This may be done as we disciple them personally. They also are taught in the local church and in a small-group home study. This growth in Christian doctrine and life plays a vital role in preparation for the baptism that follows (see verse 20).

New believers must learn and unlearn. Many come with a heavy burden of negative thinking about Christ and the Bible. Others are just ignorant, never having been exposed to any instruction about God. They must also form new habits. Paul speaks to Titus about *sound doctrine* (Titus 1:9, 2:2). The context of these verses deals with practical matters like laziness, cheating and slander. Sound doctrine flows from "the knowledge of the truth that leads to godliness" (Titus 1:1).

Who is to teach new converts from Islam? *You* are, as their friend. They may well find a traditional church uncomfortable. Even in Western lands, the Muslim community or their family may pressure them if they see them openly involved in a Christian church. 2 Timothy 3:15 tells how Timothy, Paul's disciple, knew "from infancy the holy Scriptures." Paul then notes the vital role of the Scriptures in teaching and training. In this way, new believers are led into "every good work" (2 Timothy 3:16).

You may begin a small-group Bible study and include the new believer. Perhaps just the two of you will meet alone. In these more intimate times, converts share personal burdens for prayer. They examine Bible passages and learn how to study for themselves. Bible memory helps new Christians to hide God's Word in their hearts. This keeps them from sin and gives them confidence in witness (Psalm 119:9, 11, 97, 105; cf. Revelation 12:11). We will speak more about Scripture memory later in this chapter.

Training in Doing Evangelism and Follow-up

We can do no better on this important subject of follow-up than to read prayerfully the Gospels. Jesus called His disciples so that they might be *with Him.* Notice in Matthew 4:18–22 that the concept of following Jesus is central. We see this also in John 1:35–50. The disciples followed along beside the Lord, saw His prayer life and His intense burden for others. They also caught the vision as they went out evangelizing with Him. Later, Jesus sent out the Twelve, then the Seventy-two (Luke 9, 10). The spiritual life- cycle began again: conception, birth, growth and usefulness. Jesus' disciples won those around them and trained them. No wonder! They saw how Jesus Christ did it.

Modeling a Biblical Lifestyle

A worker among Muslims spent a great deal of time in Muslim homes. The dining room table became a place of ministry. Muslims visited in his home as well. He surprised me one day by asking: "John, do you know of *any* Muslim home that is really happy? I have never seen a family where there is unity, respect, and good relations." His question surprised me. Yet my wife and I had recently come to a similar conclusion. A family may show great warmth to you as an outsider. They may help other family members and neighbors in practical ways. Joy and peace, however, are often absent.

This underlines the importance of spending time with your friend. You may want to do a study together on the patriarchs in Genesis. As new converts see these families in Scripture, with all their flaws, they will better understand God's pattern for godliness in the home. Paul instructs us concerning parents, children, husbands and wives in Ephesians 5:21–6:4. Young believers pick up much by observing Christ in our homes. They become imitators as they marry and have children of their own (Ephesians 5:1).

Muslim organizations loudly criticize the West for its godless standards. Our films, magazines and other media pour out evil. Those who go behind the façade of religion in Islam often find equal corruption "behind the veil." New and young believers are warped by *both* East and West. But as we model biblical Christianity, they observe Christ in us. They long to emulate him who "loved us and gave himself up for us as a fragrant offering and sacrifice to God" (Ephesians 5:2).

Preparing an Environment to Meet Needs

1 John 1:3 tells us: "*We* proclaim to you what *we* have seen and heard so that *you* also may have fellowship with *us*." The plurals of Paul in Ephesians emphasize the same truth. Christian growth must take place in the context of *many* believers, not just one.

Some years ago we worked with a small evangelistic team in a large French city. Said came to know Christ. All of us tried to fit the activities of our team to Said's growth needs. This young man was searching for his specific role in life. Outings, football, and endless meals of pizza, cookies and cola all contributed to this. The life of the church youth group contributed, and the church's sensitivity to his particular needs helped him to feel a part. The group drew Said like a magnet.

Sustaining by Intercession During Times of Difficulty

We have looked earlier at the significance of prayer. You may be sure that your friend will experience special difficulties. Converts from Muslim background have special questions that need answering. When they experience rejection, they may drift away for a time. They *always* need your prayers. Remember how Paul spoke more about prayer than he did about any other aspect of spiritual warfare (cf. Ephesians 6:18–20)? He referred to prayer five times in just three verses. He told us how *he,* the great Apostle, *urgently needed prayer*.

For a long time I prayed for a specially responsive group of Muslims. I did this right after lunch. Then, for some reason, I began to be less faithful in this small prayer effort. Some of my friends experienced special attacks and failures. I now feel that I did not hold them up in prayer as I should have.

Prayer is always foundational to follow-up. It played a special role in my work with Sami. He experienced family struggles coupled with an ongoing crisis in his workplace. These needs cried out for serious intercession. Occult practices in Sami's background added to the need for spiritual warfare in prayer. We saw earlier Jesus' perfect teaching to *His* disciples in John 13–16. We call this passage "The Upper Room Discourse." Do you remember how our Lord proceeded to *pray as He concluded* that teaching? We see it as He prayed for His own (John 17). Discipling cannot take place unless there is a firm foundation of intercession.

Cooperating as Your Disciple Becomes a Co-worker

Dawson Trotman, the founder of The Navigators, pointed out that we were "born to reproduce." We teach new converts personally and help them practically. We model the Christian life as Jesus did for the Twelve. Converts grow and become a part of a local church. The Ten Commandments as recorded in Deuteronomy 5:6–21 show a pattern of obedience in the life of God's people. Then Deuteronomy 6:4–9 shows us how to teach as we spend time with our friends. They see how God is *truly* One. This goes far beyond the static, theoretical unity of the unknowable god of the Qur'an. Notice carefully what follows. "Impress them on your children" (Deuteronomy 6:7). This applies to physical children, as God's people form earthly families. It also applies to those *they will train in the family of God.*

The Special Needs of Converts From Islam

A new believer from Muslim background specially needs spiritual teaching and friendship. Why is follow-up especially important, even for those of a younger generation?

The Islamic Creed drives several false teachings deep into the heart of young Muslims. "I testify that there is no God but Allah" it begins. Our problem is that this god is not the God of the Bible. God is our heavenly Father, the one whom Jesus repeatedly called "Father." The Creed goes on to state: "I testify that Muhammed is the Apostle of God." The Muslim's vision of Muhammed eclipses Jesus Christ.

The Negative Teaching of Islam.
The False Teaching of Islam
You cannot know God personally
Jesus was just a man
Jesus did not die on the cross
The Bible is full of errors and contradictions

Table 6: Some False Teaching in Islam

Bible teaching and training offers the remedy to this spiritual shortsightedness. As new believers are taught, their vision is corrected. They see spiritual realities that are far off, and not just material things close at hand. A convert needs specific *true* teaching to counter the specific *false* teachings of Islam. Matthew 28:18–20 speaks of how we should go — teaching (a participle in the original, not an imperative). The many Epistles that follow offer "corrective vision" for many practical problems experienced in living for Christ.

The Navigators are known worldwide for their burden to personally disciple men and women. They produce excellent materials, such as *The Navigators' Topical Memory System* for memorizing Scripture. God used this in my own life. He also laid deep spiritual foundations in the lives of several keen North African friends. Navigators' booklets for discipleship are also very helpful. Many use them in teaching and training a new believer from a Muslim background. Campus Crusade for Christ produces similar materials of excellent quality. Some of these studies exist in Arabic and other languages (see the Appendix for details). Arab World Ministries' Radio School of the Bible in Marseille, France, has ten courses written by a team of experienced workers among Muslims. These are available in French and Arabic.

Memorizing Scripture helps to combat false concepts planted by the enemy from early years. One Christian sister found herself surrounded by temptation. She met problems in her immediate family and opposition from her extended family. She found victory over temptation as she remembered verses she had memorized as a young believer. God's truth provided the only answer to Satan's lies.

Another Christian lady experienced deep depression. The bitter opposition of her mother and sisters fueled this inner darkness. Then God brought light in the tunnel. While on vacation she met a pastor who told her to write out fifty times the last verses in Romans 8. Her darkness faded away as the brilliant sunshine of the love of God broke through. Several Christian friends spent much time with her in prayer, encouraging her in the faith.

Some Muslims use the Qur'an as a magic charm. Those who grew up in a Muslim country surely memorized portions of it. Once, in a Christian meeting, a believer quoted verbatim a Qur'anic passage she learned as a child. God is using her today with her husband because she replaced this early teaching with God's Word.

The Strong Bonds of Family and Community

We learned in an earlier chapter of the family's strong influence. Notice the influence of Muslim families in the two examples given above. When young people from Muslim background become children of God, they literally move from one family to another. Their physical family may never again be a "tree on which to lean." Our job is simply to be there. This may mean long gaps of silence when all is going well. Periods come, however, when you will be needed. Your help may be in baby-sitting or in the practical offering of your home for a vacation spot. It may be building a relationship with their children as surrogate grandparents. Perhaps you will share good Christian books that have helped you.

One French woman did all of this with another woman for ten years! No wonder this woman came back to Christ one day. You may think: "My friend has dropped me after all I did to help." Even if this were fully true, you could continue the friendship in prayer. Then one day God uses you again in a key role. Is not the spiritual equipping of one believer in Christ worth all of this? Young women from Muslim families have special need for one good friend. New believers all need someone they can count on to listen and accept them, with all of their struggles.

Consider the story of King Saul, the first king of Israel. Several times the occult world pulled him down deeply. His reign began with spiritual pride and disobedience. It ended, for all practical purposes, with his forced interview with the witch of Endor (1 Samuel 28). More than one young Muslim convert has stumbled because of occult spiritual pressure applied by the family.

We must remind ourselves that our aims in discipling are not always reached. I wish I could have met Ahmed sooner. Teaching and example are much easier if a new believer is not in his early forties (as Ahmed). One missionary pointed out his belief that all of the disciples were quite young men when Jesus worked with them. Certainly they did not have the spiritual undertow of a mind filled with Islamic teaching. I sometimes wondered if Ahmed's family used sorcery on this dear brother. Perhaps demonic forces gripped him in areas not given over to Christ.

We need to touch on another subject here: cross-cultural marriage. A believer from Muslim background becomes acquainted with believers of different cultures through the life of the church. Relationships form, and one of these may lead to marriage. Your discipleship ministry may include prayerful advice in such a relationship. We shouldn't discourage culturally mixed marriages, but we must strongly urge young people to enter it with their eyes wide open. One of the few books dealing with this topic is *Love Across Latitudes*[23] by Janet Fraser-Smith. Many have needlessly suffered because Christian counsel in follow-up did not include this area. Who can help better than a friend?

A Pattern of Strong Personal Relationships

Many Westerners put people in formal time slots. Relationships in the East are often open-ended and informal. Because of this, a convert has a great need for *personal* follow-up. Consider again the pattern of John 1:35–39. John the Baptizer's disciples learned of Jesus through John. The gospel flowed from friend to friend (John 1:40–51).

Let's look at this more closely for a moment. The Apostle John shows us indirectly a very important principle of follow-up. Have you noticed the chain of events in this opening to a powerful, unique Gospel? First, the Apostle John links God and the Word, Christ. This link appears in a family metaphor: Father and Son. Next, John baptizes his own cousin, Jesus of Nazareth. The next day, John the Baptizer was with two of his disciples (John 1:35). Andrew, Peter's brother, was one of the two. "The first thing Andrew did was to find his brother, Simon, and tell him, 'We have found the Messiah'" (John 1:41). Then Philip found Nathaniel. In that day, family ties constituted an important part of daily life. Our world is quite different. Family ties seem to dissolve in frequent moves, job uncertainty, and divorce.

My wife and I followed up a family of Eastern background. I forged ahead with my teaching, happy to discover the Bible together with them in the beautiful Arabic language. My wife reminded me several times that the husband needed answers to some key questions.

They joined in our family events, thus seeing patterns for their own personal family. From this Christian "cell" they reached out to their Muslim family members. John baptized his cousin and Andrew found his brother, we must prayerfully seek to answer the questions of our friends. This is possible only in a personal relationship. They will then be ready to spread the gospel in their turn along personal, wider family lines.

A Lack of Opportunity to Develop Intellectual Gifts

Some Muslims in Western countries are forced to live in poor housing. They grow up with other young people who are not motivated to study. Their parents may not read the language of their new country. They may have little access to books. You should chose your program of teaching to match the ability of your disciple.

You may find that your friend grows intellectually by studying the Bible. Job asks: "But where can wisdom be found? Where does understanding dwell?" (Job 28:12). In one of the greatest passages of Scripture, he answers: "God understands the way to it and he alone knows where it dwells" (Job 28:23). New converts may have never studied anything seriously. Suddenly they are motivated, hungering and thirsting after righteousness. You will be thrilled to find that the Bible will become their first book of study.

One young American began giving conferences about dealing with youth conflicts. People began to flock to hear him. He told one large assembly in Philadelphia how he had great difficulty in his studies. Then he began to memorize Scripture. He finished at the top of his class, and then God began to use him greatly.

You never know who your disciple will turn out to be. D.L. Moody's Sunday School teacher patiently trained his boys. He never dreamed of what one would become from this discipling process. You may have heard much about the supposedly hardened, non-responsive Muslim people. God may amaze you, however, at the way He uses your disciple as this person becomes "qualified to teach others" (2 Timothy 2:2). Lebanese Nabil Jabbur described himself as "a fellow who starts but doesn't finish." Then he met an American who had confidence in him. Nabil learned the 108 verses of *The Navigators Topical Memory System*, spurred on by that confidence.

Several won to Christ in Europe have gone on to become significant leaders of God's work in their parents' countries of origin. Each of these struggled in their early schooling. Their spiritual development began with some very practical expressions of Christian love. French and Swiss missionaries taught them the

Bible, as well as job skills. They learned plumbing and carpentry. Today these young men have a radiant testimony, and a steady job.

Unique Gifts for Evangelism

New Christians from Muslim background understand their own world. This applies to the spiritual forces at work in it, as we saw in an earlier chapter. It applies also to the customs of family and religion that we explored in another chapter. Are they not the best evangelists?

Let's expand on this. Islam possesses a far reaching character. Muslims feel that they are part of a worldwide movement. This is true even if they do not practice Islam at all. A new believer in Christ from that milieu still benefits from having had this identity. Furthermore, there exists a distinct foreign feel to any Islamic community for those outside it. An immense amount of time may be needed to penetrate it. Your friend is *already* a part of it. Finally, the *second generation* has a culture uniquely its own. This begins outside of their apartments' doors. It may resemble yours, it may not. Once you cross the threshold of their home, you find another world. You will never be at home in it the way your friend will be. Since they understand their world, they are the best equipped to win it for Jesus Christ.

Discipleship and Friendship

In conclusion, I would like to review a fundamental fact about discipling. Effective teaching of a young believer in Christ draws its strength from the roots of friendship. The friendship of David and Jonathan offers a unique illustration (1 Samuel 18:1–4, 20:1–42). God worked powerfully through their spiritual alliance, a bonding of their spirits under God. That unique friendship formed a foundation for the whole kingdom of David. It also endured great testing. Any process of discipling must also go through the same fire. Notice the contradictions in this beautiful story of Scripture:

- Saul hounded and rejected David. Jonathan, however, clung to him as a faithful friend.

- Jonathan was David's best friend, yet he was also the son of David's worst enemy, King Saul.

- Jonathan's own father rejected him as a result of that friendship. Yet the friendship with David held fast.

This graphic Old Testament story demonstrates the link between friendship and discipleship. Ask God to enable you to run the risk of friendship. Then He will give you the delight of training a disciple.

The Use of Discipleship Helps and Materials

There is a wealth of material available for use in discipleship settings. Some can be used directly with your friend. Other resources are designed to stretch your thinking about the process. The Appendix will get you started on your search to discover the right tool for your situation.

The Guide to Discipleship

This is published in Samuel P. Schlorff's *Discipleship in Islamic Society*. It is a doctrinal teaching tool developed by Arab World Ministries with Arab believers in mind.

Intermediate Courses

Arab World Ministries has produced a series of ten formal Bible study courses, created particularly for the new believer of Muslim background. Their titles are:

- Overview of the Bible
- Walking in the Light (1 John)
- The Christian's Resources
- The Church
- Persecution
- The Christian's Relationships
- Basic Beliefs
- Christian Ethics
- Spiritual Warfare
- Christian Service

They are basic studies, not complicated, so interested contacts can easily sit in on the studies. Believers who are more established can do the series with a vision to teach it to someone else. Courses are available in French and Arabic but not yet in English.

The Storying Method

J.O. Terry writes about *Storying the Gospel to Muslims*. It is a chronological approach developed by Trevor McIlwain of New Tribes Mission. One chief advantage is that such a method moves beyond principles to the acts of God. You may find that your friend thinks in terms of acts, not analytical principles. Another useful tool is *The Visualized Bible*, which also gives a systematic, basic and visualized approach to teaching.

Follow-up of Children

Children often accept Christ in a neighborhood Bible club. They form an important part of the Arab Christian community in the West. How can we follow them up? Their families exert a great deal of control, as they should. This may lead, however, to cutting off contact with these fragile new believers. One answer to this is a youth center where all ages can feel at home. Another possibility is summer camp work. Here, parents can be confident that children are involved in a wholesome recreational program. Children can leave behind the harmful environment of crowded housing complexes. A systematic Bible memory program can provide special outings as a reward for achievement. Frequency in club attendance and bringing visitors may also provide points toward an outing. A full day or weekend activity will give a more intense time for modeling and teaching.

The Simplicity of Discipleship

An illustration of Huck Finn appeared some time ago on the cover of *Discipleship Journal.*[24] You may remember from Mark Twain's writings that Huck sailed down the Mississippi River on a raft with his black companion, Jim. Their relationship was unique. The magazine made that point in the picture itself. True discipling is friendship and mutual trust. Discipling finds its roots in Christ's love. The path to the mountain of success may cross the dark forest of the unexpected. Faithful prayer and persistent friendship, however, bring great fruit for God's Kingdom.

For Reflection

1. How does Jesus' example with His disciples show how I must help a new convert from Islam?

2. What are five basic spiritual needs in the life of this new believer God has given me to disciple? What biblical principles would help my friend in these areas?

For Action

1. Obtain a copy of a follow-up book, like Samuel P. Schlorff's *Discipleship in Islamic Society.* Included in this is *The Guide*, a doctrinal teaching booklet.

2. Spend some time with a Christian experienced in training a believer from Islamic background. What materials does this person use? What can you learn positively or negatively from this disciple-maker?

3. Examine *The Visualized Bible.* It is a most useful tool with large picture booklets and cassettes both in English and in Arabic. This is not just for children! My wife uses this extensively, as do several other effective disciple-makers. It is of great value in its approach to doctrine; it makes extensive use of both the Old and New Testaments.

For Additional Study

1. How are you relating your work to the local church?

2. Reflect on the family life of your friend. The pull is always real; in their case, is it positive or negative? How does your friendship reflect that?

3. How does your family life touch the life of your friend? How can you instill Christian family values in your teaching?

4. Proverbs is a good book for honing personal relationships. All of us need to grow in this area of our lives. Meditate and pray over these proverbs:
   - "Everyone is the friend of a man who gives gifts" (19:6).
   - "A friend loves at all times" (17:17).
   - "Wounds from a friend can be trusted" (27:6).
   - "As iron sharpens iron, so one man sharpens another" (27:17).

5. How can you carry out this discipling in the context of your local church? This is the team we need to back us in our ministry.

There is also the faithful teaching and worship that lays foundation stones in the lives of new converts to our Lord Jesus Christ.

6. I recommend that you read *Quality Friendship*, by Gary Inrig. How are you at friendship?

8

Muslim Converts and the Local Church

**The end result of our witness
is a bonding of the new believer
into a group — a local,
gospel-preaching church.**

Where do those won to Christ from Islam find their community? As we have seen, this idea of community (*umma*) is rooted in the hearts of young and old alike. Some remember with nostalgia the community feeling they experienced on a vacation to their parents' homeland. Others, younger, sensed this in childhood family memories with aunts and uncles. Is the local church the community they seek? Will the fact that its members speak a foreign language pose a problem? My wife and I often have the opportunity to travel to North Africa where we lived for five years. Each trip makes us more aware of these cultural and spiritual tensions.

Bonding to the Local Church

When we construct a piece of furniture, we gradually come to the point where one piece needs to fit into another. We reach up on the shelf for the wood glue. It enables us to bond the two pieces together. How can you and I serve as bridges between the new community — the local church — and the new believer in Christ? How can we help our friends *bond* with the Christian community? How do these *new persons* (2 Corinthians 5:17) then relate to the community from which they have come? How can we avoid the error of what some call *extraction evangelism*?[25]

1 John 1:3 sheds light on this recurring difficulty in witness to Muslims: "We proclaim to you what we have seen and heard, so that you also may have fellowship with us. And our fellowship is with the Father and with his Son, Jesus Christ." John goes on to speak about joy. Joy is among the rarest of commodities in the world where you and your Arab friend live. Fellowship (*koinonia*) is the natural atmosphere of the church, the visible demonstration of God's *umma*. Note the use of plural pronouns as John speaks of his witness. "*We* proclaim to you what *we* have seen and heard." Witness is a team effort. The end result of our witness is a bonding of the new believer into a group. Here our friend will find the joy of which John speaks, as well as personal significance.

Two poignant facts underline the importance of this subject. First, many new converts to Christ find themselves ostracized in some way by their families. Second, more than one of these brothers or sisters in Christ has stumbled in the process of becoming part of a local church. The church seems to be a foreign community. They may feel that they are in a kind of "never-never land," with suspicions at both borders.

Homogeneous or Heterogeneous Churches

Inevitably, when motivated Christian visitors stop by our home in France, they ask a question: "Have you thought of forming a *Muslim Convert Church* with services in Arabic?" My answer is always the same: "Yes, we have thought about it. No, we are not trying to establish one. The new believers themselves don't want a convert church." Many of us believe this because converts themselves have told us. We, with them, believe that we should make integration into a local church (where the majority language of the country is spoken) our eventual objective.

It is true, however, that there are some witnesses among Muslims who do work toward a church that is composed primarily of those who come from Islam. Perhaps a few long-time nationals of the Western country, along with other more recent immigrant peoples, make up the rest of the congregation. Foreign-born and nationals thereby blend to give the church a more international flavor.

Take my own situation in French society. If I had my choice between speaking French or Arabic, it would be Arabic. It is beautiful in itself, as are many aspects of the culture that flows around it. But when I become acquainted with my younger Muslim friends, I find rather quickly that Arabic is really a foreign language to them. This increasingly holds true for those most open to the gospel, the *second generation.*

If we represent our friends' world by a triangle, the language of their parents is at the smaller tip. The base of the triangle, however, is changing, expanding, as far as this language is concerned. Whether you like it or not, your friend is moving out into a new world. This world uses Western language in speech and thought. The triangle is growing from the bottom — youth is gaining on age. Take France, for example. Here we see a generation that grew up surrounded by the Arabic and/or Berber languages of

North Africa. Their generation is giving way to a new generation that is more familiar with French.

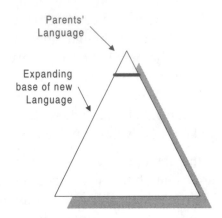

Figure 14: Changing Language Patterns

Why should we not encourage Muslim-convert churches? For the younger convert majority, the language of education is French or English. This is the basic means for communication in the mall or on the street corner. Without exception, new converts in France want to be part of a French evangelical church. They want solid links with the community in which they live. This bonding becomes more urgent as new converts experience rejection by the Muslim community.

In the new surroundings of the Christian community, the believer finds unexpected tensions. Some will find racial bias. Others will have unrealistic expectations of help from the church. The church may push the new Christian into public prominence as "our convert from Islam." Do these tensions surprise us? They should not. One of the first events in the life of the early church illustrates the same fundamental problem. In Acts 6:1–7, we discover that "the Grecian Jews complained against the Hebraic Jews because their widows were being overlooked in the daily distribution of food." Both groups lived in the same nation, so to speak, yet they manifested very different patterns of thought and action. The Grecian Jews had grown up in a Greek-speaking culture, while the Hebraic Jews came from the old, Jewish roots. Each group saw the other with jaundiced eyes. This sums up very well the conflict in the minds of many from a Muslim background. "Why don't these European or American Christians understand me?"

The early church immediately took action. Stephen, Philip, Procorus and the others moved into the highly charged atmosphere, carrying with them the perspective of their varying cultural backgrounds. These men enabled both groups to bond together, bringing practical solutions to problems that could have split the church during its infancy. So today, God raises up men and women filled with the Holy Spirit who possess an international viewpoint. This enables them to build a bridge between converts from Islam and the local churches. It is vital for you to learn about the convert's cultural and spiritual background. In this way, you may be a better bridge for your friend.

The Church as Community

The next question we need to ask is: "What *kind* of church will suit the Muslim convert in a Western country?" Let me attempt to describe the kind of church where Muslim converts will best integrate and exercise their gifts.

First, the church must be **culturally flexible** as the church in Acts 6 became. Many of the churches in France where Muslims feel most at home have a strong foreign element. By this I mean the presence of French citizens who lived in North Africa and are familiar with that culture. The churches may also have people of other cultural or national backgrounds.

An irreplaceable ingredient of a church where Muslim converts will feel welcome is that it must be an **open, caring community**. I believe two kinds of churches fit best the needs of Muslim converts in my own context in France: some Brethren assemblies and some Pentecostal churches. I have worked with a church from each of these backgrounds. Each experiences real success in Muslim ministry. They welcome North Africans and put them to work for Christ. We must always keep before us that our Muslim friend is seeking these two traits: cultural flexibility and everyday expressions of Christian love. New believers need the church body to become their new family.

Why do some churches experience more success in integrating Muslim converts than others? The two church groups mentioned above are at two ends of the theological and practical spectrum. Their effectiveness is not based on their theological belief. It is my opinion that the answer lies in the fact that they both reproduce the *umma* or community spirit so familiar to North Africans. These groups possess some marked differences. They have in common, however, a sincere concern to **minister to the whole person**. If a believer needs work, they help find it. If the apartment needs wallpaper, people appear to assist, food in hand. Where other kinds of churches have been successful, it is primarily for the same reasons.

A church's doctrinal position alone does not draw a Muslim convert. However I do not believe that the convert will find spiritual help in more liberal Protestant churches. These liberal churches may flirt with the Roman Catholic Church or even with local Islamic groups. Some Pentecostal groups, however, also actively seek ties with the Catholics; this results in moving the convert from one authoritarian unscriptural group, Islam, to contact with another — an unfortunate situation.

Converts from Islam may have difficulty finding churches where they will be happy. Louab, because he felt at home, worked hard to help construct his new church's building. Saami became a key figure in the youth and camp program of a church in southern France. Abdelkader, however, found growing unhappiness in his church group. He sensed discrimination and loneliness because of his position, being poorer than most in his church. In the case of Ridha, church leaders never asked to serve communion even though he was a baptized believer. But God blessed his faithfulness in doing an unseen task. He handled mailings for an evangelistic work based in his church.

How does church integration operate? The Apostle Paul described it well: "There is neither Jew nor Greek, slave nor free, male nor female, for you are all one in Christ Jesus" (Galatians 3:28). If you are concerned about the Muslims around you, why not talk to your pastor? Ask him to consult with the church board. Could they agree that if a Muslim believed, your church would welcome that person? You could then explore together what steps would be necessary for this to become a reality.

In downtown Marseille, France, an old Catholic cathedral decays in the midst of the Arab Quarter. Good weather graces most days in this southern port city. Go for a walk, and you will find a knot of North African men sitting on the wide steps of the church. Their presence is an interesting metaphor. We are exploring the delicate process of integrating new Arab Christians into Western churches. This process demands Christian grace and largeness of spirit. The receiving church, made up primarily of natives of the country, must welcome the converts. Converts wait, as it were, on the steps of the church. They must take initiative as well, but you and I can help them in the process. They can make important contributions to their congregations as they exercise their unique

God-given gifts. They may even become "pillars," exercising a key position in a local church.

Church Leaders from Muslim Background

Said's wife just joined him in following Jesus Christ as unique Lord of their lives. Their little family began to change spiritually as the parents grew in Christ. One day they found a newly planted Evangelical Free Church close to their apartment complex. So they began their first church-life together. We urged them to remember that churches today are "biblical" in an unexpected sense: churches today have real problems just as churches in the Bible did! Yet these churches also offer rich fellowship and teaching. All this is in stark contrast to life in the world that swirls around them. Acts 2:46 describes the vibrant, outgoing life of God's people: "Every day they continued to meet together in the temple courts. They broke bread in their homes and ate together with glad and sincere hearts." The Holy Spirit goes on to describe the result: "... praising God and enjoying the favor of all the people. And the Lord added to their number daily those who were being saved" (verse 47).

Said and Kinza most enjoyed the impact on their lives made by the pastor, Monsieur Bertrand. A humble man of God, his teaching accorded with his open lifestyle. As time went on, they also discovered some of the church problems. They faced them with maturity. My wife and I experienced great joy as we watched them drink at the source of the Word of God, "like newborn babies" (1 Peter 2:2). Then we heard that Mr. Bertrand had to leave the pastorate because of his wife's failing health. Yet our friends remained in their place, serving Christ. Now Said is active in leading evangelistic outreach. Kinza experiences at times a feeling of being ill at ease as the only North African woman in the group. Yet she would never think of leaving the church.

Would an Arab church be more suitable? At this point, Said and Kinza would say no. However, parallel fellowship with a local inter-Arab group has encouraged them greatly. None of us can predict the future shape of their experience as they continue as church leaders. Jesus Himself is building His church out of very diverse building material (Matthew 16:18). At times the spiritual progress of our friend may discourage us. Then we must remember to whom Jesus said, "On this rock I will build my church." It was Peter, with all his shortcomings. Our friends will grow because they have taken root in a local church.

I know of one city in which Muslim converts feel at home in two different small house churches. Each group includes other nationalities and each is able to adapt to the special needs of these new believers. I believe house churches can sometimes be a practical answer to the problem of converts' integration into a local church.

Christians of Arab and Berber background bring unique gifts to the Body of Jesus Christ in Europe. Racial tension is among the top issues begging for immediate solution by politicians, social workers and common citizens. High-rise apartments are plagued by violence and racial hatred. The local church becomes a model of God's solution. In the local church, Arab, European, Black African, and Asian Christians worship and work together as one. Paul faced racial crisis in the same way: "For he himself [Jesus Christ] is our peace, who has made the two [hostile groups of Jewish and Gentile converts] one, and has destroyed the barrier, the dividing wall of hostility" (Ephesians 2:14). Christ created "one new man out of the two, thus making peace," and "came and preached peace to you who were far away and peace to those who were near" (Ephesians 2:15,17).

Muslim Convert Fellowships

Some say that we should attempt to form *Jesus Mosques*. We should channel converts from Islam into an environment that resembles the local mosque. They refer not only to physical structure but even the form of the message itself.[26] We sometimes rather romantically feel that we may cure a lack of response among Muslims by some quick and easy formula.

I would insist that the **fundamental problem of resistance in evangelism and discipling is not an anthropological problem but a theological one**. We cannot make light of the heart of Islam itself. Its twin denial of the deity of Jesus and His death for our sins strikes at the heart of our faith. Muslims in Western countries often express at once some part of this Christ-denying position of the Qur'an. A quick fix will not change this attitude. We pray and God works. We proclaim Christ's name, since "no other name under heaven [is] given to men by which [they] must be saved" (Acts 4:12). Why not review the chapter on the biblical issues involved in answering Muslim objections? It will remind you that the real problem is a spiritual and biblical one.

While the new believer needs to integrate into an existing local church, people from a Muslim background need fellowship *with one another*. Perhaps you can become a catalyst, helping to introduce your friend to others of Muslim background. They may attend another church with which you are acquainted. You can play a key role in their discovery of the larger Body of Christ.

Intercultural Marriage

I do need to add a word on the delicate subject of intercultural marriage. What if our friends find life partners in the church who are not from the same cultural background? First, I recommend that you consult with an established believer of Muslim background, where possible. Second, explore with both parties the issues involved.[27] Frank communication is an important key to future success. Small-group exposure to other couples holds real advantages. Converts need time to establish their witness as true believers in Christ. Might this be merely a profession of faith in order to marry and remain in the country? This question helps to weed out wrong motives for joining the church group.

You are a part of a local church. On this basis, seek to help your friend find a place in the church's ministry. You will need to face honestly some of the problems we have spoken of here. Stress the positive ways God is using the church in your own life. Remember that the Spirit's power in the life of each believer becomes a model for change in the society where God has placed them.

For Reflection

1. Would the church I attend be a favorable place for my friend to find a home?

2. What steps can I take to make it a more hospitable environment for Muslim converts?

3. Are there any internationals in my church? Would my Arab friend feel at ease with them?

For Action

1. Consult with the leaders of your church. Could they provide a *halfway house* environment for a new convert from Islam?

2. Begin a small Bible Discovery Group in your home. Invite believers of several nationalities if possible. Encourage your friend to be a part of the group.

For Additional Study

1. Which of the churches mentioned in the New Testament best describes your own?

2. Which characteristics of churches described there would most attract your friend?

3. Read through the book of Acts. Identify the elements of the gospel that would have the most impact on the life of your friend. Pray and work to make these more a part of your church's life.

9

Communicating Love

How do we communicate love?
What does love look like?

After World War II, many people looked to the scientific community with expectations of great progress for mankind. Soon institutions and leaders would usher in an era of good government and peaceful community living. These golden ideals mock us as we look at the world of today. What ever happened to progress? Europe explodes in racial hatred. Most of the rest of the globe follows suit. If we do not war with one another, we seethe in anger within ourselves. Isaiah the prophet tells us that the Messiah is the Prince of Peace (Isaiah 9:6–7). The means of communication and understanding certainly are available in our sophisticated electronic age. Why does not love move out of our hearts to embrace those around us? Why are we unable to untie the knots of prejudice and hatred that keep peoples at odds with one another?

The answer is not hard to discover if we read the context of Isaiah's beautiful Christmas passage. In verse 5, the prophet tells us: "Every warrior's boot used in battle and every garment rolled in blood will be destined for burning, will be fuel for the fire." War and hatred are terrible realities. Yet did you notice the tense of the verb? "Will be," are Isaiah's terms. With the return of Jesus Christ to judge the earth, all wars will cease. Every day we witness the tiny but no less tragic wars of animosity and hatred on the streets of our cities. One aspect of these conflicts often catches the headlines. The ongoing misunderstanding between Muslim peoples and the Western world stands like an open sore in our time.

I firmly believe that we, as Christians, can bring an answer that never crosses the minds of most social scientists and social workers. They seek to bandage the wounds of hate. We may appear quite insignificant to ourselves and those around us. Nonetheless, we are building each day the house of our relationship to our friend. We put in place one pillar after another. We begin simply by taking the time to talk to one or two of those millions of Muslims around the world. We have learned that our message must fit their felt needs. We discover real people, hidden from the view of the Christian world around them. Our approach to them needs to include some understanding of their culture and a true respect for it.

Paul was right on target when he spoke of how the love of Christ needed to press or compel or constrain us into action (2 Corinthians 5:14). In our building metaphor, love is like the varnish on the work we are seeing God do in the life of our friend. As a rough wood surface is not attractive without a finish, neither will our witness be, however expert it may seem, without love. Paul reminds us so poignantly of this in 1 Corinthians 13. He is our great missionary example of witness to a people who are quite different from us.

We will return now to review some points that may help in our approach to our Muslim friend. Nine conduits for love will help us to win that Muslim's heart. When our witness and follow-up move along these lines, they will be fruitful for years to come.

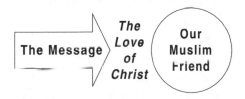

Figure 15: The Point of Entry

Notice the arrow figure. The tip represents the approach to our Muslim friend. Obviously, this point of entry is extremely important. The tip carries the initial impact of the message. We approach our friend with a smile on our face and love in our heart. That person will then be much more ready to hear what we have to say. The love of Christ compels us to speak. His Spirit within us moves us to open the conversation. We begin to share our faith. The message (the shaft) flows out toward the target of the Muslim's heart-need.

Today, emphasis on *hidden peoples* arouses much interest on the part of those who want to reach those without faith in Jesus Christ. Many imagine those outside the fold of the church as some primitive tribe in a far-flung jungle. Middle Eastern university students on a campus in your city are a hidden people, unreached for Christ. They have a specific culture that needs to be understood, for the approach prepares the way for the message. The Berber merchants in Marseille are another needy hidden people. One day I met a man from the beautiful Tunisian tourist isle of Jerba. I stepped into his grocery store in an all-French section of Marseille, not far from where my family used to live. I wondered if anyone had spoken to him before of the love of Jesus

Christ. How many *hidden peoples* live in your city?[28] As we reach out to them in love, we find that no person is hidden from the love of God in Christ.

We can think of the arrow's shaft (pictured above) as being made up of nine parts which follow the arrowhead, our initial approach. The arrow itself is a picture of sensitive, appropriate witness for Jesus Christ. There *is* no quick fix. Ask the Holy Spirit to help you respect the shape of the life and thought of your friend. We will look at nine aspects of this shape. Scripture illustrates each of them many times. They can help us discover a person hidden from the view of other Christians. Is this not what Jesus meant in His touching story of the Lost Sheep (Luke 15:1–7)?

Which of these points seem to stand out as a place of dialogue for your relationship?

Emotional Outlook	Persecution
Patience	Priority of Scripture
Parental Relations	Overcome the Myths
Power of Islam	Peace of God
Place of Women	

Paul's message of love in 1 Corinthians 13 bore lasting fruit. Why did this happen? Paul determined to "become all things to all men" in order to win them for Christ. He spoke in one way to the cultured Athenians (Acts 17); he approached those at Corinth or Ephesus in quite another way (Acts 18 and 19). Be careful of trying to put a square peg in a round hole. How do we communicate love? Saint Augustine was a North African Berber and leader in the early church. He once asked: "What does love look like?" Here are nine channels for communicating love.

The First Channel: Emotional Outlook

One evening a friend and I met a zealous Muslim student in the town of St. Martin le Vinoux. For a good while we talked very intensely in a makeshift mosque. They met in an unused building belonging to, of all things, the Roman Catholic Church. The student worked actively in the mosque. Later he attended a meeting for students at a Christian youth center. He turned out to be one of the few Muslims present. At the end of the debate, he asked if he might read the Qur'an, Surah 1. He read quite impressively, in the rhymed meter and ancient Arabic of that book. Suddenly I realized his reason for reading. He held the firm conviction that the Qur'an was God's unique word. Did not the beauty of its poetic form demonstrate this? He felt this reading would make an impact on the Christian idolaters present!

Our Muslim friends possess a unique sensitivity and creativity. They are created in the image of God. The Qur'an is officially untranslatable, with no real historical thread such as that of the Bible. How can a book like that hold their devotion? Part of the explanation is found in the simple physical beauty of Arab poetry. Even Muslims who are not Arabic speakers are impressed by the sounds of the book when read.

Hebrew poetry is quite different from the Arabic poetry of the Qur'an. Since its structure is built on correspondence of ideas rather than rhyme, the poetic books of the Bible are fully translatable into any other language. The many poetic portions of the Qur'an are not easy to translate. Yet Muslims are nearly always touched by the Qur'an. They would say that is because the Qur'an is the revelation of God. We would respond that it has only an apparent outward beauty which can never transform the moral life from the heart out.

The Psalms carry a message that is pointed not just at the ear but also the mind, will and heart. They are, nonetheless, poetry that is familiar to oriental ears. Try to read, or have your friend read one of the many Messianic Psalms (e.g., 2, 22, 23, 24). Use a translation in the Muslim's own tongue if possible. God's poetry can strike a familiar chord in the Muslim heart.

Muslim peoples possess a unique artistic sensitivity. This leads me to recommend several specific tools to use in explaining the Bible's message to Muslims:

- Audio cassettes with Christian music, but from the oriental context. One very talented young singer expresses her faith in Arabic music that has touched many who hear it.

- Visual media using a Middle Eastern design (e.g., calligraphy or pictures from your friend's homeland). *The Key of Knowledge* magazine from Radio School of the Bible is one among a number of excellent contemporary publications of this nature. Some Christian *comic books* in Arabic or Western languages may help. We need more original work, including more illustrations that depict the young person's world. Ask Muslims what they would like to see on tape or in print.

- Video cassettes, especially the *Jesus* film in Arabic and many other tongues. These images are sometimes received with objections (e.g., "Why do you show Jesus' face?"). Yet the Bible truths they convey invariably make an impact.

Speaking of feelings, we need to beware of letting our anger, frustration, or bitterness express itself. When anger is there, the wound may never heal. A Western Christian doctor lived in a Muslim country in Africa. He came to witness to that people of his faith. Then relations with another Western colleague soured. One day he was furious with the person, his anger boiling over into words and acts. He could no longer stay there, as his usefulness was ended. He quickly returned to his homeland.

It is also possible to fail to recognize the unique Eastern people with whom we are dealing, losing our sense of orientation. People of Anglo Saxon background must remember that everyone is not as reserved and taciturn as we are. We need to allow the Holy Spirit of God to guide our emotions. As the fruits of the Spirit (Galatians 5:22–23) flow through us, love, joy, and peace are expressed. Then God's Spirit touches the innermost being of our Muslim friend. What is your emotional temperature with your friend?

Remember that poetry is powerful. Do not be discouraged by the Muslim's attachment to the outward beauty of the Qur'an. Read the Bible with your friend and let the Spirit of God write it upon the tablets of the heart (2 Corinthians 3.1–3). Love flowing through the channel of emotion is like an herbal balm purchased in an Arab market. It can soothe and heal troubled hearts.

The Second Channel: Patience

An Arab proverb says: *"aS-Sabru huwwa kullu shay"* (roughly equivalent to "Patience is everything, the whole ball of wax"). One day my wife and I were waiting for a North African Christian couple with whom we were going to spend the weekend at a Christian retreat center in the French Alps. I was reading a doctrinal study by A.W. Pink: *The Sovereignty of God* (specifically a passage dealing with God's decrees). Time slipped by. I grumbled to myself: "They probably aren't able to come. We came two and a half hours down here for nothing." Finally, after about two hours, and some frustrated searching, I called the retreat center. "Try the other lot," the Director told me. We went there to find that our friends had been waiting almost as long as we had. My patience had worn thin a little too quickly. I forgot the principle of patience and waiting on God's providential leading.

> I once worked with a man named Roy Smith in Marseille. Roy showed me how to do street preaching in the crowded Arab sections of Marseille. Until then, all I knew was the discreet one-on-one witness of a restricted Muslim country. I have never forgotten a statement Roy, now with the Lord, once made to me. He said with a whimsical smile, "John, there are five rules for working with Muslims. The first is perseverance. Then the second is perseverance, as are the third, fourth and fifth."

As we launch the arrow of our message, our aim is to see the Word of God penetrate the heart of our Muslim friend. We must remember that God is not willing that any should perish, but that all should come to repentance. God, our Heavenly Father, is long-suffering. We must emulate Him.

Figure 16: The Direct Approach in Communication

Jesus speaks of the teaching aspect of our calling (Matthew 28:16–20). The work of correspondence courses for Muslims can become a vital part of our witness. The Radio School of the Bible is in touch with students from all over the Muslim world. They can study the Bible in the privacy of their own homes. Many follow these students in prayer, patiently seeing Scripture teaching come to fruition. Our Lord Jesus gave perfect teaching to His disciples in John 13–16. Yet even Jesus Christ showed us how prayer anchors that truth in the heart, as He prayed the teaching home to His students' hearts in John 17.

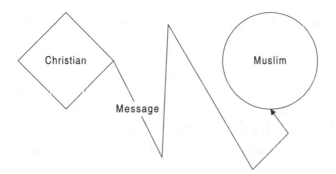

Figure 17: The Indirect Approach in Communication

There are two methods of communication: direct and indirect (see figures 16 and 17). The direct method can be represented by a straight line between us and our goal. The method most often used by our Muslim friend is indirect; we might call it *the patient approach*.

If *we* want something from someone, we simply ask the person directly. Why hesitate? After all, we know what we want. Our Muslim friends may use another method. They want to go from where they are to their goal, just like we do. But they may hesitate to seek it directly, fearing that they might be impolite or might make someone lose face. So they reach their goal by a rather circuitous route. Instead of knocking at the *front door*, they prefer to arrive by the *back door*. At least *we* see the process in that manner. This cultural pattern is seen clearly in the Bible. For example, read the story of Abraham's quest for Sarah's burial place in Genesis 23. His method of buying the cave of Machpelah is a fascinating example of the oriental method of saving face. No one in this story addressed the issue directly. The Hittites, Abraham's neighbors, did not. Abraham also used the indirect method himself. We can learn many cultural lessons from the Old Testament. These will help our message penetrate into the heart of Muslims.

The Third Channel: Parental Relations

In an earlier chapter, we examined basic cultural differences and saw the importance of the Christian *umma* or local church. Now let's carry this a step further. How can you practically implement the reality of your friend's web of relationships? The Lord Jesus worked through friends and families (John 1). How can you see the Lord work again in this way as you witness for Him?

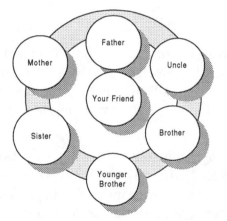

Figure 18: Web of Relationships

Remember that your friend lives and acts within a circle of relationships, not unlike a matrix or web. As you spend time in your friend's home, you will meet other members of this network, each with his or her relative influence. In the outer, more apparent hierarchy, the father is in the primary circle of influence. The son cannot borrow the car without permission from his father. That trip to the beach must await Dad's stamp of approval.

The mother operates from another circle, removed from the center because of the unique male and female relations in oriental culture. Of course, like all cultural patterns, this is constantly changing. In actual fact, mothers usually have a unique place in the hearts of their children. Their influence is reinforced by many expressions of love down through the years. Unfortunately, in some cases, her influence may take hold through her use of occult practices. In her way of thinking, she is only promoting her child's well being. According to my wife, the woman's role is preponderant in this occult aspect.

One uncle may play a very important role. This is more likely if he is older than the father. He is near the second circle. One younger brother may be far out, another in closer. Much of this description is similar to some of our own experience as Westerners. Yet the influence of the oriental family unit will probably be quite different from ours. This will remain true for several more future generations in our countries.

We need to spend the majority of our time in those activities that produce the most fruit. Face-to-face contact with people, in small groups and in family situations, will reward our efforts. Are we logging hours with Muslims? If we love them, we will be. Then we will see the mighty power of the gospel spread out, just as it did in Jesus' ministry with the Twelve. This spiritual tide began with the inner circle of Peter, James and John.

My wife and I spent some time in the country with a Christian Arab couple. To our surprise, they came to our weekend accompanied by their niece, Jezebel. (Unfortunately, she lived up to her name some years later!) We expected to spend the time as two couples. Jezebel came because she fit into their *web*. They brought her very naturally, since she was a family member. At first, I put forth to her some of the traditional answers common to Muslim objections. Gradu-

ally, however, my wife and I began to realize that these issues did not trouble Jezebel. My wife summed up our visit
succinctly: "All these Muslim young people long for in life
is to find the right spouse, and to have a peaceful, happy
home." They are not much different from many of us, are
they?

Your local church needs to support in group prayer any who have
a special gift for relating to Muslims. Perhaps the church could
even aid these witnesses financially with their entertainment and
literature expenses. Pray the Lord of the Harvest, that *such labor-
ers will be sent to the harvest of Muslims in our Western countries.*

The Fourth Channel: Power of Folk Islam

You will remember that we dealt in depth with this subject in an
earlier chapter. When visitors travel in North Africa, they see
many little white buildings with domed roofs. These are the
tombs of *awliyaa,* so-called saints or marabouts. The tombs be-
long to Muslim holy men, whose spirits are believed to still influence the living.

My wife and I often visited the home of an Algerian who
had a profound knowledge of the Qur'an, the history of Islam, and the history of Algeria. It was a pleasure to talk to
this well-educated person. He is the only Muslim I know
who has read the entire Bible in Arabic. Once I confronted
him about the saints' tombs. He replied forcefully: "You
should not downplay the importance of the Marabouts."

Ask your friend about these tombs, perhaps using a picture from a
book on a Muslim country that you found in your local library.
Prayerfully prepare a Bible passage in terms of your friend's response. Use this the next time you meet.

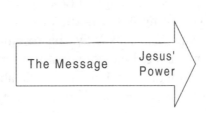

Figure 19: The Power of Christ over Satan

You seek to communicate the message of hope and power in Christ. Perhaps near the beginning you should communicate God's message on the power of Jesus Christ over the spirit world. One of my former seminary professors suggested that this approach might be a key to unlocking the heart of the Muslim today. Take time to think through several passages about Christ's power over Satan. This will be a powerful tool in communicating with a Muslim. The occult world is their world. Here in France, television programs concerning unusual (often occult) events fascinate many Muslims.

You notice a Qur'anic verse on the wall, or a picture of Mecca as you visit in a Muslim home. A "Hand of Fatima" hangs on your Muslim neighbor's new car. These are not just tokens or decorations; they represent a real fear, and an attempt to protect themselves from those who wish them evil.

What are some ways you could bring out the power of God and of His Son, our Lord Jesus? Several experiences may illustrate this.

- Our friend Nasser had a year of university studies. He was well aware of magic writings, fetishes, and other occult objects. He regularly welcomed us in his home. Yet occult subjects often lurked in the background of our conversations. Seek to tell openly a story of Jesus' casting out a demon and watch your friend's reaction. Show how Jesus also has the power to forgive sin.

- What role do sacred magic books play with Muslim youth? I was visiting in the home of a young Muslim in the French Alps. In many ways he resembled a typical older teen in France. Our conversation turned to magic books and formulas. He began to talk about a special family book high up on a shelf in the living room. After some tactful persuasion, he finally took it down, and gave it to me. I examined the large volume with great interest. The writing was old Qur'anic script. The book quite obviously contained magic formulas. This reminded me of the books burned in Acts 19:17–20. Read this portion with Muslims and notice how they react.

- Magic fetishes may be holding a Muslim from serious consideration of Christ. *Pif* is a popular French comic magazine which targets children. Some years ago, it published a waving hand that could be placed in a room or in a car. It seemed innocent enough, until we saw it appearing as a protection symbol in various places, including an Arab friend's nice Ford. A discerning French pastor was very upset by the tenor of the magazine.

Remember that behind much of the power of the occult world is *fear in the heart*. People will not easily talk about this aspect of their lives. But it is very real. When you speak of a spiritual victory God has given you, your friend may open up to you. Muslims sometimes fear that we will ridicule them for speaking of the occult. *They* know that the spirit world is very real. So should we. Scripture tells us that "perfect love drives out fear" (1 John 4:18).

The Fifth Channel: Place of Women in Islam

Muslim culture is a man's world. Visit cafes and markets in Arab sections of Western cities. You will notice the near total absence of women. Some years ago a Moroccan women's rights group published the magazine *Lam Aliif.* The title is a word play on *aliif lam*, which is the definite article in Arabic. Together, these two Arabic letters mean "NO!" This group of women sought to improve the status of women and establish their movement within a Muslim country. Some twenty-five years later, however, the status of women does not seem to have changed much in Islam. The outward observer sees very little difference, especially in popular sections of large cities. Muslim young people in Western cities have a very different individual lifestyle, but this usually comes into conflict with their parents.

Remember this as you go into your friend's home. You need to be careful not to misjudge their culture. Note the role of male leadership in the lives of the patriarchs. Some of Paul's statements in the New Testament also underline God's use of male leadership in the Christian church. These issues may be affected by culture. A careful reading of Acts shows the growing role of women in the New Testament church. Our problem is that we often go to the opposite extreme. We may be unable to appreciate many positive elements of our friend's environment.

How can you elevate women to their rightful and God-given place? Certainly you can pray for change. As you discover the forms of male-female relations in your friend's milieu, you should remember the following general guidelines:

- If you are a man relating to a woman in the family circle, show respect, be reserved and discreet. In conversing with older male Muslims, you may ask, "How is the home?" Do not ask: "How is your wife?"

- If you are a woman relating to a man in the family unit, it is often proper to avoid direct eye contact. Certainly you should avoid the kind of casual, friendly touching that is common in the West. If you are to see a Muslim man whom you do not really know, you might wonder if his interests may be for more than just acquaintance. Try to go with a Christian brother.

- Remember the problem of mixed marriage that we referred to earlier. A major advance of Islam in the West is through Muslim marriage with Western women.

- All of us should observe the family and note how those our age dress. Sometimes we will not want to follow their example. In other cases, this will show us if our dress is improper. The guideline is to forget your own culture and try to best fit into theirs. Keep in mind the biblical injunction of "being all things to all people."

The Sixth Channel: Persecution

One expatriate Christian witness was a relative newcomer in a Muslim country. He was stunned when a lead article appeared in the Arabic language newspaper, attacking him and his friend. To his amazement, however, a local Christian wrote a careful, biblical answer to the attack. Another major newspaper published this answer.

You may think, "That kind of attack is normal for a Muslim country, but it would never happen here." No, even in the West there can be real hardship on the part of those who receive our message. As we deliver the truth, we must think of the cases of persecution in the New Testament. At times we need to adjust our message with the book of Acts. Muslim fundamentalists visited a North African believer several times. This Christian had been very bold in his witness. They threatened him and his family. They often spied on him and phoned him in the middle of the night. His spiritual light went out and has never since been rekindled. Some Muslim authorities sweep down on new believers like vicious birds of prey.

> Another brother, a Tunisian, lived in France and desired to travel overseas. His father had expelled him from the home because he "followed the Europeans." This brother was not at all sure he could get a new passport. His father had his old one. Even if this young man went to the embassy, he thought his father would intervene. He could blackmail the son, since he had not served in the army of his homeland. The son could be arrested.

Only those who live in daily situations like these can understand the extent of the pressure. Remember that the message you bring may be accepted at great cost. A favorite passage in facing open opposition is Psalm 2. "Why do the nations conspire, and the peoples plot in vain?" asks the Psalmist. Then he goes on to talk about the Son. Islam rejects Christ's Sonship, saying it is just some teaching Christians have invented. Yet we read in Psalm 2:4, "the One enthroned in the heaven laughs." Then God gives the appeal to accept Christ in unique terms. "Kiss the Son, lest he be angry and you be destroyed in your way" invites God the Father (Psalm 2:12). Once I was entertaining a person whom I suspected of trying to infiltrate our work; he was certainly a troublemaker. I read him this psalm very early one morning. Gradually he stopped coming to interfere with my ministry.

Here are some suggestions for handling both overt and more subtle forms of persecution:

- Be careful what you say about your church and Christian organizations as you visit in a Muslim home. There is much suspicion and some of it is warranted. Police organizations from their own country often try to keep tabs on them. Some families fear local authorities as well. They may want to avoid the discovery of some petty crime practiced by a family member.

- Remember Nehemiah: He concentrated on his *job* and not on the enemy. Even when his enemies tried to compromise him by meeting together, he refused. We also need to look at the Lord and get on with the job. We should not try to fight opposition in the flesh.

- Do not let fear keep you from speaking. I once traveled by train to a Muslim country with a number of other young people. I had advised them to be very discreet in handing out literature. Among them was a zealous German brother who was very tall and easy to see in a crowd. To my initial horror, he spoke openly right in front of others on the train. Yet God used his testimony, and we experienced no police problems.

- There is a place for real wisdom and discretion. In an Arab section near where we live, I hesitate to have a market Bible stand. I would rather approach people on a personal level.

- Remind yourself that Arab people as a whole are not unkind and hostile. In many ways, they have endearing traits that have attracted my wife and me for thirty years. You may find it helpful to share some of your own struggles in living in a different culture. I sometimes tell Arabs in my Western country of how my family moved when I was a child. People in that other part of America lived very differently from our family's normal customs. As I grew up, my foreignness became the focus of taunts by some around me. Sharing helps your Arab friends to see their own struggles in a new light.

- We should begin by recognizing the *true source* of opposition to us and our message. Jesus focuses on the world's opposition in the Upper Room Discourse (John 16). The world system raised a venomous head to attack the person of our Lord Jesus. Muslims may attack Jesus as Son of God and Messiah. Behind them, however, stand the world and the devil. But remember that Jesus Christ possesses all authority. He will prevail.

The Seventh Channel: Priority of Scripture

I will just touch on this since the subject was addressed when we examined a biblical understanding of the Arab peoples. Remember Charles Malik's remark. We can never understand the conflict in the Mideast without referring to the conflict between Isaac and Ishmael in the Bible. A biblical understanding leads to genuine love touching and warming the heart of Muslims near us.

Take a moment to review Genesis 16:1–6. Sarah came from the people of God, yet she mistreated Hagar, her servant. Hagar came from outside the Chosen People. In this passage, however, it is Hagar who seems to be the more spiritual one. Note also later revelations of God to Hagar. Sarah at times appears listless spiritually. Now read Genesis 16:7–16. Does this text support this conclusion? What does Genesis 16:10 tell you about God's blessing on the Arab peoples, who consider Hagar to be their mother?

Perhaps this week you will meet a Muslim acquaintance for coffee. Your conversation will turn to God and His revelation to us. It is likely that as you return home and reflect on the issues, you will feel a keen burden for the spiritual condition of this person.

Soon a passage from the Bible will come to mind. A few days later you meet again for an outing with friends. You are amazed to find that your understanding of the doctrine under discussion is much deeper. Jesus, our hope, gives you an expectation that the Holy Spirit will bring this Muslim to know Him. God's love once again reaches both you and the Muslim through the Scriptures.

The Eighth Channel: Overcome the Myths

How wise are we in understanding this Muslim friend that God has placed on our path? Three great myths concerning Islam are prominent among Christians in Western countries. Wisdom demands that we identify and avoid them.

Myth 1: All Arabs are Muslim fanatics and are against Western nations.

We cited Charles Malik, the Lebanese Christian, in considering the preceding channel. He is just one of many Arab believers in Jesus. Many Palestinian evangelicals have suffered for Christ. Some have witnessed faithfully to Muslims. There are important Christian minorities in countries like Iraq, Egypt, and Syria. You may have to seek to understand your Muslim friend's different position on the Middle East and other world events. The person is not a fanatic at all; just different from you!

Myth 2: It is impossible for a Muslim to become a Christian.

Consider two facts: the open witness of Kabyles in Algeria and the growth of regional gatherings in France of Christians from Muslim background. These are just two among countless examples. They prove that the second myth is, in fact, only a myth.

Myth 3: I am not qualified to witness to Muslims. An expert, someone who speaks their language, is required.

This one often follows the destruction of the first two myths. Do you remember the story of the young man from the beginning of this manual? He believed this myth and asked me to come to witness to his Muslim student friend. Yet Jacques was the expert in the final analysis. No matter how little he knew, he had become a friend to this young Muslim doctoral candidate. A Spirit-guided and empowered relationship became a platform for the gospel. Jacques bore effective witness to the Savior he loved. God's secret weapon in winning Muslims to Christ in Western countries surprises most of us. This weapon is the average church member who befriends the Muslim on the steps of the church.

Whenever you have the opportunity, seek to dissolve these myths in your church. Remember a great watchword of witnesses to Muslims: "Your labor in the Lord is not in vain" (1 Corinthians 15:57–58).

The Ninth Channel: Peace of God

This principle flows out of the reality of persecution and the primacy of Scripture. Muslim converts face persecution. So will we as we bear witness to the truth. When we begin to understand what the Bible says about Arab peoples, we also will see how today's friendship can easily dissolve in tomorrow's hostility.

Saul had a long-term enmity toward David. We may find a similar enmity as we go to the Muslim world. Perhaps we will experience real hatred from those around us for the first time in our lives. There is also a more subtle form of opposition experienced by Jesus which we may also feel. It is a greater or lesser measure of scheming, just as we see in the Old Testament record when Saul plotted against David. There is nothing like oriental scheming in its cleverness and deadliness. Yet in Saul's case, love would also surface at times. One example is when Saul called David his own son, regretting what he had done. Saul's opposition seems demonic, at least in part. It began with an evil spirit in his early reign and ended with the witch of Endor as his life drew to a close (1 Samuel 18–28).

We will experience the ambivalence of some Muslim friends we seek to win. We then enter into Jesus' sufferings, as Paul puts it. He speaks of the *fellowship of Christ's suffering* in Philippians 3:10. We will know that privilege as well.

Turning Initial Enthusiasm to Faithful Commitment

You will see initial enthusiasm to yourself and to your message. But you seldom find faithful commitment in the end. We looked at the emotional aspect of the Arab's nature. The Arab's enthusiasm may lead you on; the welcome seems so warm, surely eternal friendship will result! Here in Toulouse, it is said that the inhabitants will give you the hand but not the arm. Warmth goes only so far. This is true of some Arab peoples, too. Exploding friendship one day may be followed by deflating hostility the next. Those of us who come from the southern part of North America know something of this in our own culture.

What can we do to counter this humanly depressing situation? We must remember David's love for Saul. David's love was faithful, in the very face of hatred. Our Lord Jesus loved His enemies, saying: "Father, forgive them." Check your own motives. Does the love of Christ constrain and compel you to reach out in love to your Muslim "neighbor"?

For Action

Review the practical suggestions made in discussing the different channels. Put one of these into practice with your Muslim friend this week.

For Additional Study

Why did Paul's message of love (as expressed in 1 Corinthians 13) bear such lasting fruit? Was it because he was willing to "become all things to all men" in order to win them for Christ? He spoke in one way to the cultured Athenians in Acts 17; he spoke in another way to those at Corinth or Ephesus in Acts 18 and 19. Study Paul's approach in these passages.

Afterword

I trust you have enjoyed this voyage we have made together. I am sure the gospel has become more clear to you as you have shared it with another. Some of the biblical passages we have seen and the spiritual issues with which we have grappled are probably now more in focus. Doubtless your prayer life has deepened as you have interceded for your Muslim friend. You know more of spiritual conflict, but also of the person near you whose existence you perhaps ignored before. Love has flowed through numerous channels and has touched that special person God placed near you as your neighbor. Is your friend still far off from Christ, to all appearances? Persevere. Share your vision with a fellow Christian; form a weekly prayer team, asking God to give you one whom you may disciple into his or her place in the local church.

The aim of this toolbox is to see Muslims in Europe, North America, and worldwide find the true Messiah and Savior, the Lord Jesus Christ. What joy will then be theirs as they join that host of others of their kin in offering praise before the Throne of God! What joy will be yours and mine as we see how the Holy Spirit made us His instruments in this world-changing event! Islam in its more violent form often shocks to attention those of us in the West. I praise God for increasing numbers from East and West who have given up their personal comfort and ease to befriend this beloved people, introducing them to Jesus. Then we will enter into the same mission and program undertaken by God our Father. David describes this so well in Psalm 2:

> *I will proclaim the decree of the Lord:*
> *He said to me, "You are my Son;*
> *   today I have become your Father.*
> *Ask of me,*
> *   and I will make the nations your inheritance,*
> *   the ends of the earth your possession..."*

Have you proclaimed the plan of forgiveness of sin in Christ to a Muslim near you? If so, you have in a real sense a new inheritance. You join with Christ who said, "As the Father has sent me, I am sending you" (John 20:21). Would you like to write me and share your joys and discoveries? Let me know how this book has helped you. Write me, in care of the publisher, Middle East Resources, P.O. Box 96, Upper Darby, PA 19082.

In a sense, this toolbox is neither fish nor fowl. Each of the nine chapters appeared separately in some other form. I have come to call it a manual, rather than a book. Yet this guide is more than that. I anticipate it will serve the reader longer than a temporary seminar or a summer outreach.

Several years ago I attended a Europe-wide conference where I met people of many nationalities. We were united by two elements. The first was a God-given concern to reach Muslim peoples in Europe. Everyone there also reflected the lingua franca of English. This enabled us to communicate, even if for many this was their second language. As I listened to these men and women of God, the Lord began to nudge me with an idea. Why not bring together some of the material I had shared in various forms in the past? I praise God for my friends listed below. Their help was essential in seeing the work to completion.

I am grateful to Abe, Muriel and Wen for hammering out the initial shape of the book from the perspective of Muslims in France
and North Africa. (I will not give their full names since they remain active in the Muslim world,). A number of other colleagues
with Arab World Ministries contributed suggestions and ideas.
Nelly Vos spent many hours on the meticulous task of translation
from Arabic into French, which resulted in clarifying the English
text as well. (She did say that she enjoyed it!)

On the North American side, Dr. Phil Steyne and others at Co-
lumbia Biblical Seminary helped me to focus my thoughts on paper when this was a project for a MA degree. Several other
friends worked on errors both in detail and in the overall structure. Dale Eklund provided aid indirectly through keeping me lit-
erate in the use of a computer. A special thanks to Bill Saal, who
came into the picture more recently and gave up a part of his sab-
batical to put in final form the English edition. Finally, my son
John D. Haines (not to be confused with his father, John F.) did
the art work. I trust this will delight the reader as much as it has
those who have seen the drawings in their original form. Some of
these are based on pictures taken by my teammate, Ron.

It is impossible to thank the "shadow contributors" to this manual. My wife and I have passed our 25-year milestone of work in
France. I owe so much to French church members and pastors,
summer-team seminar participants, Arab brothers and sisters, as
well as a number of Muslim friends. They helped to shape and
correct my prayers and thoughts about reaching Muslims in
Western countries. These pages come *from* them in a real sense. I
anticipate now that they will return *to* them for that greatest of
aims:

*Why do the nations conspire
and the peoples plot in vain?
The kings of the earth take their stand
and the rulers gather together
against the Lord and against his Anointed One.*

*I have installed my King on Zion, my holy hill ...
Therefore, you kings, be wise ...
Kiss the Son, lest he be angry
and you be destroyed in your way ...
Blessed are all who take refuge in him* (Psalm 2)

Your Brother in Christ,

John F. Haines
Toulouse, France

Appendix: Arabic Transliteration

Name of Letter	Transliteration	Pronunciation
'alif	aa	fair
baa'	b	big
taa'	t	tell
thaa'	th	think
jiim	j	measure
Haa'	H	no equivalent
khaa'	kh	loch (Scottish)
daal	d	dead
dhaal	dh	then
raa'	r	rolled r
zaay	z	zoo
siin	s	sew
shiin	sh	shall
Saad	S	no equivalent
Daad	D	no equivalent
Taa'	T	no equivalent
DHaa'	DH	no equivalent
'ayn	‘	no equivalent
ghayn	gh	no equivalent
faa'	f	fool
qaaf	q	no equivalent
kaaf	k	kitten
laam	l	love
miim	m	mask
nuun	n	never
haa'	h	happy
waaw	w,uu	weld, food
yaa'	y,ii	yell, breeze
Hamza	’	no equivalent

Resource List

Cross-Cultural Understanding and Missions

Bernstein, Richard. *Fragile Glory: A Portrait of France and the French.* New York: A. A. Knopf, 1990.

Charnay, Jean-Paul. *La Vie Musulmane en Algérie.* 1965; reprint Paris: Presses Universitaires de France, 1991.

Duvignaud, Jean. *Tunisie: Collection Atlas de Voyage.* Lausanne: Rencontre, 1965.

Govan, Stewart I. R. *The Love That Was Stronger, Lilias Trotter of Algiers.* London: Lutterworth Press, 1958. A challenging example of the kind of consecration it takes to win Muslims to Christ, and the usefulness of a wide understanding of their culture.

Hiebert, Paul G. *Anthropological Insights for Missionaries.* Grand Rapids: Baker, 1985.

Howard, David M. *Moving Out: The Story of Student Initiative in World Missions*. Downers Grove, Illinois: InterVarsity Press, 1984.

Inrig, Gary. *Quality Friendship: The Risks and Rewards*. Chicago: Moody Press, 1981.

Mahmoody, Betty. *Not Without My Daughter*. London: Corgi Press, 1989.

Mallouhi, Christine. *Mini-Skirts, Mothers and Muslims*. Turnbridge Wells, UK: Spear Publications, n.d. Distributed by STL Distributors, PO Box 300, Carlisle, Cumbria CA30Qs, UK. In spite of an overly dramatic title, this book contains many helpful insights to those foreign to Muslim culture.

Mernissi, Fatima. *Beyond the Veil: Male-Female Dynamics in Modern Muslim Society*. Rev. Ed. London: Al Saqi, 1985. The author is a Moroccan university professor and sociologist. This is a much-misunderstood area of relations between westerners and Muslims.

Olson, Bruce E. *Bruchko*. Carol Stream, Illinois: Creation House, reprint 1985. While relating to a "primitive" indian culture, the depth of the author's sacrifice and identification is remarkable, if unique.

Patai, Raphael. *The Arab Mind*. New York: Scribner, 1976. A classic analysis of Arab culture and perspective.

Richardson, Don. *Eternity in their Hearts*. Ventura, CA: Regal Books, 1981. Also available in French. (L'Éternité dans leur coeur. Québec: Jeunesse en Mission, 1984.)

_____, *Peace Child*. Glendale, CA, G/L Publications: 1974. Also available in French. Both of these books, as Olson's, speak of tribal cultures, but contain many truths that apply to any witness from one culture to another.

Smalley, William A. *Readings in Missionary Anthropology II*. Pasadena: William Carey Library, 1984.

Tapiéro, Norbert. *Manuel d'Arabe Algérien Moderne*. Second Edition. Paris: Librarie C. Klincksieck, 1978. Tapiéro spoke the Algerian dialect like a national. At the end of this work 15 dialogs help us understand aspects of life in Algeria before independence. The progressive learning texts also give many insights. Much has changed, yet "the more things change, the more they remain the same."

Islam

Andrae, Tor. *Mohammed: The Man and His Faith*. New York: Harper Torchbooks, 1960.

Cragg, Kenneth. *The Call of the Minaret*. New York: Oxford, 1956. Both scholarly and understandable, Cragg is a gripping writer, in spite of the fact that some of his views are not those of this writer.

_____, *This Year in Jerusalem*. DLT, 1982.

_____, *The Event of the Qur'an*. Allen & Unwin, 1971

_____, *The Mind of the Qur'an*. Allen & Unwin, 1973

_____, *The Wisdom of the Sufis*. Sheldon, 1974

_____, *Muhammad and the Christian: A Question of Response*. Maryknoll: Orbis Books, 1984.

Farah, Caesar E. *Islam: Beliefs and Observances.* Woodbury, New York: Barron's Educational Series, 1970. A comprehensive work, suitable as a text for serious group study, as well as a reference work.

Geertz, Clifford. *Islam Observed.* New York: Yale University Press, 1968.

Gilsenan, Michael. *Recognizing Islam.* New York: Pantheon Books, 1982. This is an anthropologist's view, with several case studies.

Hamoiri, Andras and Ruth, trans. *Introduction to Islamic Theology and Law.* By Ignaz Goldziher. Princeton: Princeton University Press, 1981.

Pullapilly, Cyriac K. *Islam in the Contemporary World.* Notre Dame, Indiana: Cross Roads Books, 1980.

Schoun, Frithjof. *Understanding Islam.* London: Mandala Books, 1976.

Taylor, John B. *The World of Islam.* London: Lutterworth Press, 1971; reprinted., New York: Friendship Press, 1979.

Von Grunebaum, G. E. *Muhammadan Festivals.* New York: Henry Schuman, 1951.

Witness among Muslims

Abdul-Haqq, Abidyah Akbar. *Sharing Your Faith With a Muslim.* Minneapolis: Bethany Fellowship, Inc., 1980.

Budd, Jack. *Studies on Islam.* 1967; Reprinted Northants, England: Stanley L. Hunt, 1981.

Campbell, William. *The Qur'an and the Bible in the Light of History and Science.* Middle East Resources, n.d.

_____, *The Gospel of Barnabas: Its True Value.* Rawalpindi, Pakistan: Christian Study Centre, 1989.

Chai-Lien, Liu. *The Arabian Prophet: A Life of Mohammed from Chinese and Arabic Sources.* Shanghai: Commercial Press; Revell (distributor), 1921.

Elder, John. *The Biblical Approach to the Muslim.* Fort Washington: WEC, 1978.

Goldsmith, Martin. *Islam and Christian Witness.* London: Hodder and Stoughton, 1982.

Hanna, Mark. *The True Path: Seven Muslims Make Their Greatest Discovery.* Colorado Springs: International Doorways, 1975.

Ibraham, Ishak. *Black Gold and Holy War.* Nashville: Thomas Nelson, 1983.

Jadid, Iskander. *The Cross in the Gospel and in the Qur'an.* Basel, Switzerland: Center for Young Adults, n.d.

McDowell, Josh. *The Islam Debate.* With Ahmed Deedat. San Bernardino, California: Here's Life Publishers 1983 (Two audio tapes). Many Muslims and Christians have heard of Muslim Ahmed Deedat's debates with various people. McDowell gave both answers and a striking demonstration of Christian love.

McCurry, Don, ed. *The Gospel and Islam.* Pasadena: William Carey Library, 1979.

Miller, William McElwee. *A Christian's Response to Islam.* Phillipsburg, NJ: Presbyterian and Reformed Publishing Co., 1980.

Parshall, Phil. *Beyond the Mosque: Christians Within Muslim Community*. Grand Rapids: Baker, 1985.

_____, *New Paths in Muslim Evangelism: Evangelical Approaches to Contextualization*. Grand Rapids: Baker, 1980. This book contains some interesting suggestions, even if we might not agree with all his suggestions.

Pfander, C.G. *The Balance of Truth*. 1910 Revised, Light of Life Austria 1986. The Arabic edition is available in a trilogy, the first volume of which deals with the issue of possible corruption in the Bible. An older book, it is still the author's favorite for witness to educated Muslims.

Saal, William. *Reaching Muslims For Christ*. Chicago: Moody Press, 1993. A greatly expanded handbook that has been in use for many years among North African Muslim peoples. Applies to all Muslims.

Schlorff, Sam. *Discipleship in Islamic Society*. Marseille, France: Ecole Radio Biblique, 1981.

St John, Patricia. *Until the Day Breaks: The life and work of Lilias Trotter, Pioneer missionary to Muslim North Africa*. Bromley, Kent: OM Publishing, 1990. Trotter was the inimitable artist-missionary, trained under Ruskin, yet who became a pioneer to the little known peoples of Algeria. This was in a day when single women's initiatives to Muslim peoples were a rarity. She led the way for all of us who followed, including the author of her story. St John wrote *Star of Light* and other books for children and adults relating to the Muslim World.

Tisdall, Sinclair, ed. *MaSaadir al-Islaam* (The Sources of Islam). Rikon, Switzerland: The Good Way, n.d. In it the author reveals a number of the contradictions and inaccuracies in the Qur'an. It has the advantage of being in Arabic. Few such works exist today because of violent Islamic reaction.

Zwemer, Samuel M. *Childhood in the Muslim World.* New York: Revell, 1915. This is an old work, older even than most by Zwemer, called "The Apostle to Islam." It still reveals many secrets to those working with Muslim families and children today.

_____, *Studies in Popular Islam.* New York: Macmillan, 1939.

_____, *The Moslem Doctrine of God.* 1905; Reprint Gerrards Cross: WEC, 1981.

The Occult World and its Relation to Islam

Anderson, Neil T. *The Bondage Breaker.* Tunbridge Wells: Monarch, 1993. Also in French.

_____, *Victory over Darkness.* Tunbridge Wells: Monarch, n.d. Also in French.

Bakhtiar, Laleh. *Le soufisme: Expressions de la Quête Mystique.* Pays-Bas: Le Seuil, 1977. An English edition also exists: *SUFI, Expressions of the Mystic Quest.* This book unveils such secrets as the use of numbers, dreams, astrology, and mystic poetry in"the Voyage toward God" (pg. 32). Sufism is a commentary on the heart cry for more than the often distant god of the Qur'an.

Brooks, Thomas. *Precious Remedies Against Satan's Devices.* Carlisle: Puritan Paperbacks, 1993. Brooks is a Puritan who is relatively easy to read. The intense spiritual conflicts going on in the England of his day revolved around doctrinal compromise. Sound doctrine is also a key to winning in our true *jihad* of teaching, prayer, and taking Christ's authority. These truths are not dated.

Bubeck, Mark I. *The Adversary: The Christian Versus Demon Activity.* Chicago: Moody, 1975. Practical insights for those involved in spiritual warfare, which applies to our witness to Muslims as well. A suitable sequel to this is his *Satanic Revival.*

_____, *Overcoming the Adversary.* Chicago: Moody, 1984. Using the resource of prayer to gain victory.

Collinson, Bernard. *Occultism in North Africa.* Marseille, France: Radio School of the Bible, 1977. A booklet by a faithful witness who has lived among Muslims for long years, and knows this aspect from personal experience. Also in French.

Dickason, C. Fred. *Demon Possession and the Christian.* Chicago: Moody Press, 1987.

Imtiaz, Ahmad. *Ritual and Religion Among Muslims of India.* New Delhi: Manohar, 1981.

Parker, Russ. *Battling the Occult.* Downers Grove, Illinois: InterVarsity, 1990.

Parshall, Phil. *Bridges to Islam: A Christian Perspective on Folk Islam.* Grand Rapids: Baker, 1983.

Penn-Lewis, Jessie. *War on the Saints.* Ninth Ed. New York: Thomas E. Lowe, Ltd., 1973.

Steyne, Philip. *Gods of Power.* Houston: Touch Publications, 1990.

Subhan, John A. Bishop. *Sufism: Its Saints and Shrines,* Lucknow: The Lucknow Publishing House, 1960.

History of North Africa and its Church

Cooley, John K. *Baal, Christ, and Mohammed: Religion and Revolution in North Africa.* New York: Holt, Rhinehart, and Winston, 1965.

Daniel, Robin. *This Holy Seed. Faith, Hope and Love in The Early Churches of North Africa.* Harpenden, U.K.: Tamarisk Publications, 1993. This large recent volume is written by one with solid experience among Muslims. It is good reading to associate with Cooley's volume (above).

Steele, Frances R. *Not in Vain.* Pasadena: William Carey Library, 1981.

Notes

1 For example in Surah 9 we often find the expression *Allah wa rasülihi*, "God and his Prophet," that is, Muhammed.

2 In the Creed, the names of Allah and Muhammed are separated by one letter in Arabic, the weak semivowel *waw*. Furthermore, a number of statements in *The Hadith* (Islamic traditions) give glory to Muhammed similar to that attributed to Mary in Roman Catholic traditions.

3 The common Muslim name in Arabic for Jesus. Some Christians object to the use of this Muslim designation since it may tap into the pool of ideas that Muslims have about Him. But we can use it, at least temporarily, since otherwise some Muslims will not understand the identity of the person about whom we speak. The Arabic Bible calls him yesuu'a.

4 This is chronological Bible storying used in a culturally acceptable way. See *Inter-Link* letter, No.10, Nov.11, 1994 (H. W. Reimer, Limoges, France).

5 Muslims often tell us: "Yes, the Prophet Jesus did miracles. We want to tell you about our Prophet, Muhammed. He is the great Seal of the Prophets. He brought us a miracle book: the Qur'an." We can gently remind them, however, that the Qur'an is written in 7th century Arabic. Then we may add: "You say that Islam is universal. You also say that the Qur'an cannot be translated. But it is in a language that many people groups in Muslim countries do not understand. Non-Arab Muslims are expected to be profoundly marked by the Arabic language and its lifestyle. Why do you force other peoples to learn a foreign language in order to worship the true God? The Bible, on the other hand, is translated into languages of peoples all over the world. They are not forced to pray in a tongue they don't use every day.

6 Obviously the answer to the Hagar-versus-Sarah question makes a difference in the way we think and act. From time to time I run across a near hatred of Arabs from those of whom I would expect it the least — evangelical brothers and sisters. This often stems from a surface view of God's promises concerning

the future for the Jewish people. And it makes me think of the quote by Julie Andrews in the film *Sound of Music,* "Let's start at the very beginning; it's the very best place to start." Our beginning is the book of beginnings and foundations: Genesis. The picture illustrates the various pieces of the puzzle of our relationship to our Muslim friend. They will fit together only as the foundation is correct (See Figure 4).

[7] In fairness, I must add that the definition of *Arab peoples* is a complex affair. Not all ethnologists agree that they are descended from Ishmael and Hagar, as many Muslims believe. My own opinion comes by inference from Scripture and the geographic placement of the ancestors of the Arabs. In perspective, however, the example of Hagar reminds us not to generalize. She was Egyptian; yet at that time the Egyptian peoples were not *Arab* in the limited sense of the term. For an excellent discussion of this subject, see Georges Houssney's article in *ReachOut,* Vol. 3, Nos. 1 & 2 (June 1989). He comments on the *Table of Nations* in Genesis 10: "If [the Muslim claim of Meccan settlement by Ishmael and Hagar] is true, Ishmael would be the father of only a fraction of the Arabs of Muhammad's time."

[8] Reticence to express what we really believe and internalize is, of course, common to most of us. It is more of a problem in our relation to our Muslim friends, however. They may feel a need to carry on a verbal Jihad or holy war. This is because we seem to be attacking their faith. Many Muslims also have a real gift with words and enjoy debate just for its own sake.

[9] This issue is treated at length in a number of books. See *The Balance of Truth,* pp. 41–125; *Reaching Muslims for Christ,* pp. 83–102.

[10] The key issue focused on here is the liberal critics' late date of John. Robinson ended up accepting an early date, thus agreeing with what evangelicals had been saying for years.

[11] If you are so inclined, study a book on church history to see if this theological issue came up in the centuries prior to Islam. The first four objections mentioned here were major issues in pre-Islamic church history. Our Enemy then went on to embody them in a world religion, Islam, so that many continue to struggle with them today.

[12] This is a term used to denote the children of immigrants, raised entirely (or nearly so) away from their parents' nation of origin. They tend to adopt the ways of their new land, sometimes losing touch with certain cultural values and the first language of their parents.

[13] Betty Mahmoody, *Not Without My Daughter.* London: Corgi Press, 1989.

[14] The word *Haraam* comes from the Arabic tri-literal root *H-r-m*. Our word *harem* comes from the same root. It means to set apart to God, sanctify, and can refer not only to women but also to objects.

[15] Samuel Zwemer, *Childhood in the Moslem World*. New York: Revel, 1915 (an old book but with lasting insights).

[16] You may want to ask yourself: "Are there any biblical substitutes for some of these family practices?" If your friend is rejected by the family or community, this will become especially important.

[17] We should examine the world view that underlies Muslim folk beliefs. A number of good books are available, such as *Bridges to Islam*, by Phil Parshall (Baker Book House, 1983), the writings of Bill Musk and the booklet *Occultism in North Africa* by Bernard Collinson (Arab World Ministries, 1977). Other general surveys of occultism are useful, such as Philip Steyne's *Gods of Power* (Touch Publication, Houston, 1990). Such spiritual searching will provide us with insight that will help us, and our friend, to be "more than conquerors."

[18] The ideas of French existentialist authors like Albert Camus (raised in Algeria) and Jean-Paul Sartre lead youth in Europe along a different path. Here too, however, a personal God has no practical presence. His revelation and demands never filter down to the real level of daily life.

[19] September 1984, p. 25.

[20] "Popular Islam: The Hunger of the Heart" in *The Gospel and Islam*. Edited by Don McCurry. Monrovia, CA: MARC, 1979, pp. 172ff.

[21] Mark Bubeck has carefully explored this in his writings, such as *The Adversary*. See also Russ Parker, *Battling the Occult*. Downers Grove, IL: InterVarsity Press, 1990.

[22] Waldron Scott, formerly of The Navigators, provided another excellent definition during a seminar conducted in Morocco in the late 1960s: "Follow-up is the practice of devoting continuous personal and individual attention to a believer from the time of his spiritual birth until he is established in a mature, reproductive Christian walk."

[23] Janet Fraser-Smith, *Love Across Latitudes*. Middle East Media.

[24] Issue Fifteen, 1983.

[25] This means pulling them out of their community of family and friends as a dentist would *extract* a troublesome tooth.

[26] A North African friend carries out a very effective Christian ministry to Muslims. He believes that this idea in itself is an imposition from Western orientations in the social sciences, rather than a biblical attempt to "sit where they sit." I would add that a missionary method may apply in one part of the Muslim world and not be appropriate elsewhere. Arabs won to Christ in the European scene fall into a very different category.

[27] A helpful workbook on intercultural marriage is *Love Across Latitudes* by Janet Fraser-Smith.

[28] With other friends who witness to Muslims, I am wary of an improper application of the so-called *redemptive analogy* principle. In his book *The Peace Child*, Don Richardson describes a unique ceremony of making peace among the Sawi people of New Guinea. He relates how God led him to use this ceremony to explain how God's Son came to bring us peace. The Sawi people knew the ceremony. Richardson went from the known of this ceremony to the unknown of the gospel. We must be careful not to apply wonderful stories like this without reflection on our relationship with our Muslim friend. This *bridge* worked for a primitive, tribal people who were isolated from external influences. The very civilized Muslim peoples of North Africa and the Middle East have a very different background. Beware of seeking a quick fix. On the other hand, God can certainly use some world event or a remarkable conversion to cause a great turning of Muslims to God. Many of us look at the fall of communism and feel that God may bring about the fall of the Islamic world system in a similar manner.

Index

Other Books Available From Middle East Resources

The Qur'an and The Bible in the Light of History and Science

by Dr. William Campbell

This book is an excellent apologetic for the Christian faith that addresses many of the objections raised by Muslims. The book is a response to the French doctor, Maurice Bucaille, whose book, *The Bible, The Qur'an and Science* is very popular among Muslims. **$12.00.** (English)

Understanding the Muslim Mindset: Questions About Islam

answered by Sam Schlorff

This little booklet is a compilation of Questions and Answers about Islam, responded to over the years by Sam Schlorff in a regular column of the same title in Arab World Ministries newsletter, *UPDATE*. A valuable resource for those who are dealing with some of the key issues in understanding ministry among Muslims. **$2.95**.

Use the Order Form in this book to purchase your copies today.

Order Form

Phone orders: 1-800-447-3566, ext. 7310 (Call for quantity discounts)

Fax orders: (610) 352-2652

On-line orders: books@awm.org

Postal orders: Middle East Resources
PO Box 96
Upper Darby PA 19082

Title	Price	Quantity	Amount
Good News For Muslims	$8.95		
The Qur'an and the Bible in the Light of History and Science	$12.00		
Understanding the Muslim Mindset	$2.95		
		Subtotal	
		Shipping	
		Total	

Shipping (surface rate; please call for faster UPS delivery):

Total Cost of Purchase	Shipping
Up to $5.99	$4.00
6.00-$20.00	$5.00
20.01-$50.00	$6.00
50.01 and up	8% of total purchase

Ship to:

Name: _____

Address: _____

City: _____ State: _____ Zip: _____

Telephone: _____

E-mail: _____

Call toll-free and order now